Holloway Halstead Frost

On a Destroyer´s Bridge

Salzwasser

Holloway Halstead Frost

On a Destroyer´s Bridge

1. Auflage | ISBN: 978-3-84607-350-6

Erscheinungsort: Paderborn, Deutschland

Erscheinungsjahr: 2015

Salzwasser Verlag GmbH, Paderborn.

Reprint of the original, first published in 1930.

Holloway Halstead Frost

On a Destroyer´s Bridge

Salzwasser

ON A
DESTROYER'S
BRIDGE

U. S. S. "TOUCEY"

ON A
DESTROYER'S
BRIDGE

By

HOLLOWAY H. FROST
COMMANDER, U. S. NAVY
AUTHOR OF *We Build a Navy*

1930
UNITED STATES NAVAL INSTITUTE
ANNAPOLIS, MD.

Composed, Printed and Bound by
The Collegiate Press
George Banta Publishing Company
Menasha, Wisconsin

Many of the methods of coöperation between the bridge and engineer department, which are so essential to the efficient operation of a destroyer, were worked out in conjunction with Lieutenant (J.G.) Elliott B. Strauss, engineer officer, U.S.S. *Toucey*.

TABLE OF CONTENTS

CHAPTER

    I. Destroyer handling as an art.................. 1

    II. Some preparatory measures................... 4

    III. Shoving off from other ships................ 10

    IV. Backing away from another destroyer.......... 12

    V. Going ahead from another destroyer........... 21

    VI. Leaving a tender or oiler.................... 24

    VII. Leaving a dock............................ 25

    VIII. Maneuvering in narrow waters................ 31

    IX. Cruising in formation....................... 47

    X. High-speed maneuvering..................... 52

    XI. Engineering operation...................... 60

    XII. Landing alongside another destroyer.......... 66

    XIII. Landing alongside large ships................ 79

    XIV. Landing alongside a dock................... 84

    XV. Anchoring................................ 94

    XVI. Securing to a buoy........................ 105

    XVII. Towing a large ship........................ 109

    XVIII. Handling a destroyer in heavy weather and among field ice........................... 112

    XIX. Handling boats............................ 117

    XX. Conclusion............................... 120

Chapter I

DESTROYER HANDLING AS AN ART

To maneuver a destroyer in restricted waters or crowded harbors; to handle her alongside other vessels or docks in strong winds and uncertain currents; to pilot her through intricate channels or dense fogs; to keep her accurately in position in close formation at high speeds day or night; to bring her through gales in the open sea or in an exposed anchorage—that truly is an art.

There are a variety of definitions of this much-used word. Also, some ancient sage—I forget who—said that all definitions were dangerous. Still we must have one. By a combination, rearrangement, and modification of several we have constructed one to suit our purpose. It reads:

> Systematic application of knowledge and skill—acquired by study, observation, and experience—in effecting a desired object.

If the desired object in this case be further defined as the *safe, smart, effective,* and *economical* operation of *a* destroyer we may all start off with a clear idea of the purpose and scope of this narrative.

The most expert destroyer captain, if an ordinary mortal, even as you and I, will freely admit how often he has been fooled by some trick of wind or current. He will tell you how frequently dangerous situations have confronted him with startling suddenness. Usually, it is true, he will admit that he should have foreseen what happened; but hindsight is a lot easier than foresight. In some cases, however, the causes of his deception will always remain a mystery. Even when things look easiest, watch out! Never let your guard down; and always keep delving into the principles which underly this intricate art.

Scarcely a week of active operation will pass without teaching some lesson—one which, if properly learned and remembered, may on occasion prevent serious damage or forestall unpleasant inquiries.

Just as in other arts—navigation, aviation, horsemanship, or even war—there are many systems or schools of destroyer handling. Each captain develops his own system, mostly by that ancient and none too satisfactory method of trial and error. For any given situation there may be several effective methods, and no claim is made that ours are superior to others. But even if a captain believes he has a method to meet any situation which may arise, it may be helpful to have a few alternate methods in reserve should some unusual condition make his usual method ineffective. Only an officer thus fortified to meet every phase of a swiftly changing situation, no matter how deceptive, may be called an expert in the art of handling destroyers. And such expertness is only relative. It has no limit. Even the best falls far short of perfection.

The methods described herein have been developed by *study*, *observation*, and *experience*—to quote from our definition. All have been proved by over four years of destroyer command. During this period a detailed record has been taken of each day's operations, with special reference to the mistakes made and lessons learned. To make doubly sure of basing the methods upon *first-hand practical experience* we purposely have avoided consulting any other papers on the subject.

The description of methods is supplemented by a rather complete series of diagrams. No attempt has been made to draw them exactly to scale or to reproduce hydrographic features directly from a chart.

While the captain is learning his rôle on the bridge, the engineer officer must be studying and developing a similarly intricate and equally important art below. For the safe and economical operation of the boilers, engines, and auxiliaries in proper coördination is a task requiring a high degree of knowledge and skill, as well as much theoretical planning and practical experimentation. By this we mean not the merely technical methods of using to advantage the individual pieces of machinery—important though that phase of engineering may be—but the art of combining the operation of these individual pieces into a general set-up for the entire plant. This set-up must effect not only the safe and economical operation of the engineer department, but also must provide such reserve power and flexibility as will meet all reasonable demands from the bridge. The adjustment of such conflicting factors naturally requires the closest coöperation between captain and engineer. Each must understand thoroughly the task of the other and interchange all the information necessary for working in complete unison.

CHAPTER II

SOME PREPARATORY MEASURES

For the captain to utilize his knowledge and skill to best advantage he must have the means of translating decision into instant and effective action. Certain arrangements to accomplish this purpose must be discussed briefly at this point.

To gain the advantage of uniformity and habit all maneuvering alongside docks and other vessels or in restricted waters must be done at one standard speed. This is fifteen knots. If another standard speed is used at sea the captain should change it to fifteen knots as soon as formation is left while entering port.

It will be found very convenient to designate such pressures for the backing turbines as will give approximately the following results when one engine is going ahead and the other astern:

One-third ahead and one-third astern.........one knot sternway
Two-thirds ahead and one-third astern........one knot headway
Two-thirds ahead and two-thirds astern.......one knot sternway
Standard ahead and two-thirds astern ....one knot headway
Standard ahead and full astern..............one knot sternway
Full ahead and full astern..................one knot headway

This arrangement of backing pressures allows the ship to be twisted—if we may be allowed to coin this idiom—with three different powers and with either headway or sternway on the ship. It gives the captain definite advance knowledge of how he may expect the ship to move with any given combination of engine speeds. It gives him a check on the accuracy with which the throttle men answer his signals. In this respect absolute accuracy is essential and must be demanded. Not only must signals be answered quickly, but the exact pressure or revolutions must be used and the acceleration to the indicated speed effected at a constant and moderate rate. Throttle men frequently use too much steam in starting and reversing turbines when maneuvering. This is a very dangerous practice. Steadiness and accuracy should be given a distinct priority over speed. In particular, signals for one-third speed should be answered very slowly and carefully when making a landing. These speeds are used for niceties of adjustment and special accuracy is essential. Often the stem or the propellers will be only a few yards away from obstructions and excessive power may result in serious damage. The captain can help out by planning his maneuvers in such a way as will not require sudden reversals or variations of speed. He never should send such a rapid succession of signals that the throttle men get hopelessly behind in their execution and confusion becomes inevitable. In destroyer handling, as in war, "order, counter-order, disorder," is a true maxim. It shows the crew that the captain does not know his job and destroys his influence as a leader.

If by reason of falling steam or other engineering casualty the speed signaled from the bridge cannot be made, the throttle men should move their annunciators to the speed the engines actually are making. The engineer officer should inform the captain when speed can be resumed. The captain should not bother the people below with inquiries. Patience is a virtue he would do well to cultivate.

The engine-revolution indicators on the bridge and in the engine-rooms are essential to the proper maneuvering of the ship. They should be kept working, even if exact calibration is impracticable. In the engine-rooms they will be of great assistance to the throttle men when the engines are maneuvered rapidly and when they are accelerated from low to high speeds. On the bridge they give the captain instant warning of any incorrect operation of the engines and an opportunity to rectify such errors.

A very good man should be stationed at the annunciators on the bridge. He should be familiar with the captain's maneuvering methods and should report immediately any operation of the engines, either by the captain or the engine-room, which appears erroneous. When one's mind is trying to keep abreast of the developments of a veritable three-ring circus it is easy to say "port" instead of "starboard," particularly when stern-way is on the ship. Sometimes when there is headway on the ship and you are ordering the handling of lines, it is possible to forget that you have an engine backing. It is an added safe-guard if the annunciator man will sing out that such is the case when the time comes for it to be stopped. He also should watch the revolution indicators and report any discrepancy between the speeds signaled and those actually being made.

In case of failure of the engine-room annunciators the bell pulls should be used. You will find engraved on a plate by them the same old system of signals that existed when Farragut expressed his contempt of the torpedoes and told Jouett to go "four bells." A new system should be devised which will correspond to the speeds now in use. The following is a satis-factory one:

One bell......ahead one-third		Repeated......astern full
Two bells.....stop		Four bells.....ahead standard
Three bells...astern one-third		Repeated......ahead full
	Five bells......ahead flank	

If the annunciator from engine-room to bridge is in operation these bell signals should be answered with it.

When maneuvering alongside vessels or docks it is convenient to order rudder angles in multiples of 5 degrees, except that full rudder should be limited to 28 degrees. For maneuvering in formation standard rudder usually is 22 degrees, but in case there is some lost motion between the rudder indicator and the rudder it should be increased one or two degrees so as to turn with the same radius as the other ships. For slight modifica-tions while turning it is convenient to ease the rudder to 20, 18, or 15 degrees and to increase it to 25 or 28 degrees.

The helmsman should warn the captain if the course ordered appears to be in error or if the rudder apparently is left on longer than necessary. An amusing instance of this occurred during a night search problem off the Shantung promontory.

We were fourth ship out from the coast. The searching course as ordered was converging on the coast line, so that the three inboard ships had to ease out. After several hours a turn to the rear was ordered by radio. As we started to execute this order—running without lights at twenty knots—all three inboard ships were sighted close aboard in quick succession and attention was focused on them most intently. I remarked afterward that we seemed to be a long time turning that 180 degrees, only to be informed that we had turned through 540 degrees. Had the helmsman made an inquiry as to whether we really desired to perform such a peculiar maneuver, probably it might have been avoided.

It is essential that the smoke telegraphs be kept in working order. Just rewire them for twenty volts and there will be no further trouble. Have a man on watch fifteen minutes before getting under way and keep him there fifteen minutes after the engines have been ordered secured. This will greatly increase boiler efficiency and save you some of those aggravating "Foxes."

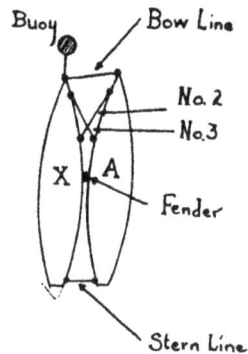

FIG. 1.—Mooring lines.

Four lines only are necessary for the handling of a destroyer. In Fig. 1 our ship is A. It is secured alongside ship X, which in turn is secured to a mooring buoy. The four lines are:

Bow line—a 40-fathom 5-inch line running across from our bullnose to the bullnose of the other ship.

No. 2—a 40-fathom 5-inch line leading aft from our forward forecastle chock to the after forecastle chock of the other destroyer.

No. 3—a 40-fathom 6-inch line leading forward from our after forecastle chock to the forward forecastle chock of the other destroyer.

Stern line—a 40-fathom 5-inch line leading from our chock just forward of the depth charge rack across to a similar chock on the other destroyer. It is far better to concentrate the attention of all personnel aft on the proper handling of this line than to endeavor to use others, which are of little, if any practical value. This system has been used for many years and with entire success.

A large cane fender is between the two ships amidships. This fender should be entirely above the guard rails and at least one foot clear of the water. Should it ride between the guard rails it will quickly be chewed up. If it gets into the water it will soon become oil-soaked and smear up the side in a most annoying fashion. When the fender becomes somewhat worn and flattened out, weave a layer of old boat-fall line over it. Thus its usefulness may be prolonged indefinitely. It has been found convenient to stow the fender in the well deck. Raise the gangway davits a few feet and they will be perfectly designed for hoisting out the fender by means of a small tackle. This method has been found much more satisfactory than stowing it on top of the midship deckhouse, where there is no means of getting it up from over the side, unless you can induce some one to take the chance of performing an unauthorized alteration for you. Your arts of persuasion will have to be more effective than ours.

When secured alongside a tender for overhaul, a 50-fathom, 7/8-inch wire hawser should be run through the bullnose to a forward chock on the tender. In this case or when secured to a dock additional lines may be used aft.

It is important to have rapid and accurate communication with the people manning the stern line. An officer should be posted on the after deckhouse in charge. Telephone communication between him and the bridge is very desirable. If not available, a system of rings on the voice-tube call bell has been found to work well. This is as follows:

— —	Man voice tube	— · —	All clear
· · —	Single line	— — —	Shift colors
— ·	Slack line	· — ·	Take in slack
— — ·	Throw off line	· —	Hold line
	— — — — —	Secure	

Often it is impracticable to tell the officer aft exactly how to handle his line. The captain's attention may be centered on other things or it may take too long to get the order through. For these reasons, the officer aft must be allowed much freedom of action. His mission is to keep the ship parallel. This he accomplishes by holding his line when the stern is out and slacking it when the stern is in. He must be careful to keep the line out of the propeller, warn off boats, and keep the bridge informed of floating logs which the propellers are liable to foul. When the stern is close to other vessels or obstructions he must continually inform the captain how many yards or feet he has to spare before touching them. Such reports are essential to the proper handling of the ship.

An officer may be placed in charge of the forecastle when getting under way or mooring, but, as the captain gives the orders directly to the men handling each line, this is not essential. A good boatswain's mate will fill the bill nicely. A special cylindrical rope fender should be made for use on the forecastle, about three feet long and fifteen inches in diameter. There are lines at each end. The fender is put over vertically, with its top about a foot above the edge of the deck. It will save many a stanchion. If your own landings are so good as never to require such a fender, perhaps the fellow who lands alongside of you will not always be so good.

Chapter III

SHOVING OFF FROM OTHER SHIPS

There are two methods of leaving from alongside another ship: backing away or going out ahead. Under normal conditions the former is much the safer. There are three principal reasons for this:

(a) Our inboard propeller is soon clear of the other ship.

(b) This propeller sends a strong current between the ships which tends to wedge them apart.

(c) There is no danger of fouling the anchor chain of the other ship or the buoy to which she is secured.

Fifteen minutes before getting under way the captain should come on the bridge and make that well-advertised estimate of the situation. Here is a wonderful opportunity to put into actual practice War College knowledge and to gain skill in practical, as opposed to theoretical, estimation of the various factors upon which the decision should be based. These should include the wind, current, yaw of the ship, positions of other ships, and the location of buoys, shoals, or obstructions which may interfere with the maneuver. If another destroyer shoves off first observe carefully the method used and how it works out. Then decide upon your own plan of action. Try to imagine all the various contingencies which may occur in its execution and think out the best measures to meet each. Of course, Clausewitz told us long ago that whenever you prepared for three cases the fourth always would occur. So be ready for some queer trick of wind or tide or some faulty handling of the engines which you cannot foresee. For purposes of instruction explain your estimate of the situation to the officers on the bridge. State your initial plan and the variations you have thought out to meet all possible developments. If these involve any unusual measures explain them to the engineer officer and the officer in charge aft.

Before commencing the maneuver the boiler steam pressure should be raised close to the safety valve settings. Except in unusually difficult situations where prolonged high-power maneuvering is expected one blower will be ample. In case of urgency one boiler is sufficient for a simple maneuver. In case of emergency skilled handling can make it sufficient for a difficult maneuver.

In leaving another ship or a dock, first get the ship carefully into the proper position, and then execute one continuous maneuver ahead or astern. You can't stop halfway, and the quicker you get clear the better. It's like stealing second—he who hesitates is lost.

CHAPTER IV

BACKING AWAY FROM ANOTHER DESTROYER

First assume the simplest conditions: no wind or current and no obstructions in your way. Take a look at Fig. 2. Place your ship *A* parallel to the other destroyer *X*. If your bow is in before you start backing it may scrape the other ship, for the current from the inboard propeller will force the sterns apart, which in turn will tend to bring the bows together. Therefore have your ship parallel.

Hoist the inboard anchor, still stocked, on deck. If you secure daily along the same side of another destroyer, it is convenient to unstock the inboard anchor and keep it permanently on deck, with its outboard fluke inside the edge of the forecastle deck. Its chain may be left unshackled from the anchor, ready for running out to the mooring buoy. The outboard anchor is kept stocked and ready for letting go in case of an engineering casualty or other emergency.

When lines are singled and all is ready, signal the officer stationed aft to throw off the stern line. Keep all the forecastle lines taut. From your station on the inboard edge of the bridge watch the stern line come in. See that it is clear of the inboard propeller. Wait for the signal "All clear," as a final check. Then back one-third both engines (*A*). When the ship starts moving astern cast off all the forcastle lines. Watch the ship's bow—whether it moves out or in. If one engine is started before the other or they are accelerated unequally to the assigned speeds or pressures, it will put a slight twist on the ship. First attempt to correct this tendency with the rudder

Buoy

X   A

Screw
Current

⅓   ⅓

B

⅔

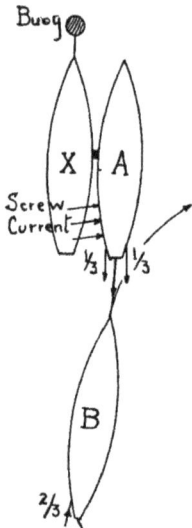

Fig. 2.
Backing away.

—putting it inboard if the bow moves in. Then stop the appropriate engine, continuing to back the other one-third. If this still does not produce the desired result increase the speed of the backing engine. As a last resort go ahead with the engine you have stopped. As it is a very simple operation to back away from another destroyer, it is seldom that it is necessary to apply more than the first two of these corrective measures, but it is well always to think them out in advance. When clear, stop the outboard engine; put the inboard engine two-thirds ahead (B). When the ship starts ahead, move the rudder outboard. When pointed well clear and in the desired direction, go ahead two-thirds both engines and ease the rudder.

To make the problem a bit more difficult, assume a rather extended shoal astern (YZ in Fig. 3). The destroyer group (X and A) is yawing considerably in the wind —or, it may be, the current. This yaw provides a means of avoiding the nearer part of the shoal Y, but will not be sufficient to permit your ship A to clear the more distant part of the shoal water Z.

First, spring your bow in well toward the other ship with the bow line and capstan.

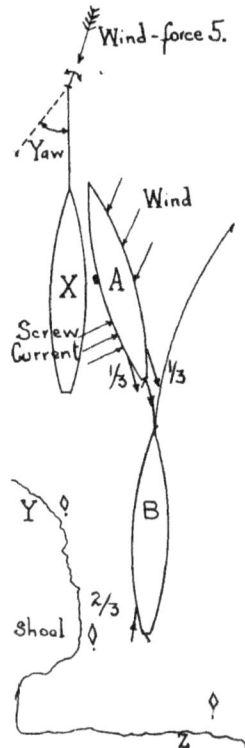

FIG. 3.—Backing away with shoals astern.

Now this is contrary to the procedure we have just advised, and gives early in our study an example of the necessity of judging each situation on its merits. It is true, as before stated, that this procedure introduces the possibility of your bow being swept in against the other ship by the wind or current when you back away. However, it points the ship 15 degrees farther away from the shoal and gives the maneuvering room which alone makes the maneuver possible.

Next, wait patiently until the end of the yaw is reached. You have been watching the motion of the ship for the last fifteen minutes and know that when your stern points just outside the buoy near Z you have reached the end of your swing in this direction. At the right instant cast off all lines quickly and back one- or two-thirds, with the rudder inboard slightly to counteract the tendency of your forecastle to be swept in (A). If you have timed your maneuver correctly ship X will be commencing her yaw away from you and your screw current will give her an additional push. The inboard rudder also will keep you from getting too nearly broadside to the wind or current—with the consequent possibility of being swept on shoal Y. When your bow clears the stern of the other ship, stop the outboard engine and put the inboard engine ahead two-thirds. When sternway is lost shift the rudder (B). Watch your stern at this stage of the game. If it gets too close to the shoal, ease the rudder as necessary or steady the ship. By this time ship X probably will be at the other end of its yaw and well out of your way. Remember that your propeller blades reach below the keel. If they hit a rocky bottom there will be another instance of an irresistible force striking an immovable body. This has been tested out and found not good for the propeller.

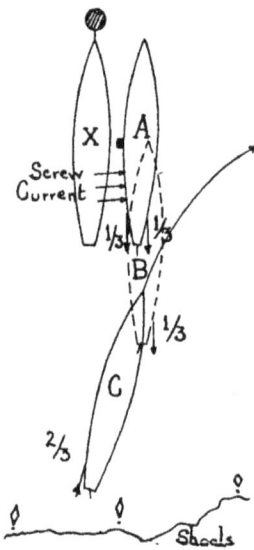

FIG. 4.—Backing away from a destroyer with shoals astern, alternate method.

If the shoal is too wide to be avoided in this manner, bring your bow out a bit (A in Fig. 4). Back both engines one-third. After going about one-third the ship's length, stop the inboard engine and put the rudder inboard (B). This will turn the ship sharply under the stern of the other destroyer, a maneuver which will be assisted by any wind or current from ahead. Next stop the outboard engine and go ahead two-thirds or standard with the inboard engine (C). Shift the rudder when the ship gains headway. Straighten out when pointed clear. This method is practicable if there is as much as seventy-five yards of good water under the stern before shoving off. Somewhat more is shown in the figure for purpose of clarity.

A strong current from ahead presents no difficulty in backing away from another destroyer; in fact, it usually is an advantage. Have the ship parallel before shoving off. In this case it is particularly disadvantageous to have your bow in before commencing the maneuver.

A current and wind at right angles may present a difficult problem. One such situation occurred in the Wangpoo River at Shanghai (Fig. 5). A group of four boats was riding to a buoy against a flooding tidal current of three knots. A force-five wind blew from the port beam. This swung the sterns to starboard so as to bring the current about 30 degrees on the starboard bow. The left ship X was secured to the buoy. The right ships began to back off in turn. The first

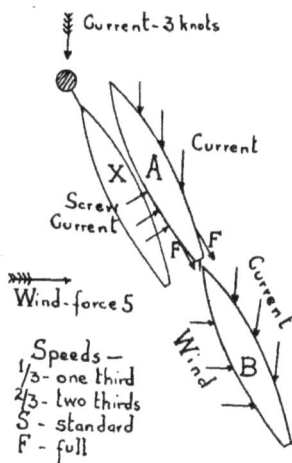

Fig. 5.—Backing away with wind and current at right angles.

backed only one-third speed. It was pushed in most dangerously and missed touching by only a few inches. The second ship was pushed in so strongly that she had to stop after having gone astern half a ship length. She was pressed by the current against our propeller guard and held in this dangerous position for a long time. Through skillful handling she was gradually worked clear.

We had, of course, been watching carefully the maneuvers of the two outboard vessels. Their results had convinced us that some new and radical method must be used. The engineer was instructed to start two blowers and warned to have the steam up to the button. When full-speed astern was signaled he was told to spin the throttles wide open, or, in popular idiom, to give her the gun. The ship was laid parallel and when all was clear aft full speed both engines was rung (*A*). The strong screw current wedged the ships apart and most effectively counteracted the river current which was pushing them together. The ship went clear by a wide margin (*B*). While as a general rule it is undesirable to use high power in maneuvering alongside other vessels, there are some cases where it is essential. This was one of them.

Now doubtless the reader will ask a very pertinent question: Why did we not have the port ships leave the group first? While I do not recollect that the division commander expressed an opinion on this point, my answer would be that it probably would increase rather than diminish the difficulty of the problem. We did not have an opportunity of proving this point at the time, but years later a very similar situation confronted us in the York River. Again the wind and current were at right angles, but this time the current was only about one knot, much weaker than that rushing

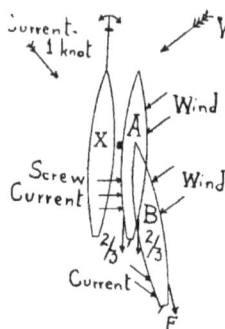

FIG. 6.—Backing away with strong wind and weak current at right angles.

tide which sweeps along the Wangpoo. On this occasion our ship was on the side toward the wind. The destroyer group, two vessels in this case, was lying midway between wind and current (Fig. 6). The wind, of course, was blowing us strongly against the other ship. As the current came from beyond that ship it had little pushing-off effect while we were still alongside (*A*). However, as soon as the stem would clear (*B*), it was evident that the current would catch it, thus swinging the bow in. This swing would be accentuated by the wind effect on the high bow and the tendency of a destroyer to back into the wind. These facts warned us that the situation had dangerous aspects. These were not improved by the fact that only one boiler was ready, and there was no time to wait for the other.

Steam pressure was raised to the safety valve setting. The engineer was warned to be ready, so far as he could be with one boiler, for high-power maneuvering. The rudder was put 10 degrees inboard and both engines were backed two-thirds (A); it was considered impracticable to use full speed with one boiler. Despite these precautions, when the ship gained sternway the bow was swept in very rapidly. The inboard engine was stopped. The rudder was moved hard inboard. The outboard engine was backed full (B). Even these radical measures were only partly effective. The bow cleared the other ship's side by about a foot—or less. Kicking the inboard engine ahead two-thirds would have eased the situation; but it is doubtful if steam would have been available for its use. The best way to avoid the unfavorable effect of wind is to get way on the ship. Even a gentle breeze has a strong effect on a vessel without way on. But work up to five knots' speed and the wind effect becomes almost negligible.

Fig. 7.— Backing away with inboard engine only.

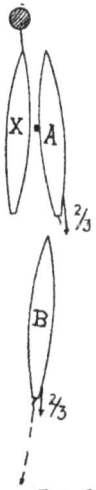

Backing away is more difficult when you have only one engine available. If you have only the inboard engine (Fig. 7), there is danger that your bow will scrape against the midship deckhouse or boat davits of the other ship. I saw it happen recently. Get the bow well out and stern in—about five feet between propeller guards. Put the rudder inboard 20 degrees. Back the inboard engine two-thirds (A). As soon as there is good sternway on the ship, stop the engine to avoid its twisting effect, which will tend to swing the bow in. When clear, go ahead with the inboard engine and full outboard rudder (B).

Fig. 8.— Backing away with outboard engine only.

When the outboard engine alone is in commission get the bow well in (Fig. 8). Put the rudder outboard. Back two-thirds on the outboard engine (A). Shift the rudder when you have gone astern half the ship's length (B). You will then pass under the stern of the other vessel. Continue the maneuver as may be necessary. When the outboard engine only is available, it will usually be preferable to go out ahead, as the inboard engine normally is not required for this maneuver.

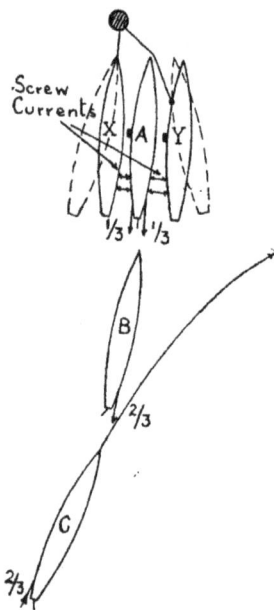

FIG. 9.—Backing from between two destroyers.

Backing out from between two destroyers is much easier than it looks. It is a comparatively simple maneuver if the throttle men handle their engines accurately. See Fig. 9 for the normal form of this problem. One outboard destroyer X keeps her anchor chain to the buoy. The other, Y, leads a mooring line from her after forecastle chock around the bow of the center vessel A to the buoy. The inner end of this line should be led to the capstan in readiness for heaving in quickly. When all is ready the center vessel casts off lines on both sides and backs both engines one-third (A). The screw currents push out the sterns of the outboard ships. If you can keep the ship steadied there will be ample room for you to slide out between. If the bow goes to either side this tendency should first be corrected with the rudder. If this will not steady the ship increase the backing speed of the appropriate engine to two-thirds or even full.

If you desire to turn to the right, stop the port engine when your bow clears the other vessels, back the starboard engine two-thirds and put the rudder left (B). When you have gained about a ship length of open water, stop the starboard engine and go ahead two-thirds port. When headway is gained, shift the rudder (C).

The center vessel is much less likely to receive injuries in this maneuver than the two outboard ships. As soon as the center vessel starts to back out, ship Y should begin heaving in on her line to the buoy, so as to avoid being swept aft by wind or current. As the sterns of both outboard vessels will be swept out by the screw currents, their bows will be swung in together. This tendency will be increased by the wind or current from ahead. Thus it is impracticable to keep their forecastles from coming into contact. If these are at different heights some stanchions may be carried away. Have your special cylindrical rope fender ready to put over. It is invaluable for such situations.

The problem becomes more complicated, or even dangerous, if there are other vessels or obstructions directly astern. On one occasion a destroyer A had to back out between two other vessels X and Y secured to a mooring buoy at Charleston. (See Fig. 10). A group of three destroyers Z was secured to another buoy directly astern. The distance between buoys was two hundred yards. A 3-knot current from ahead did not simplify the problem. When ready to commence the maneuver, both engines were backed one-third (A). When the bow was abreast the

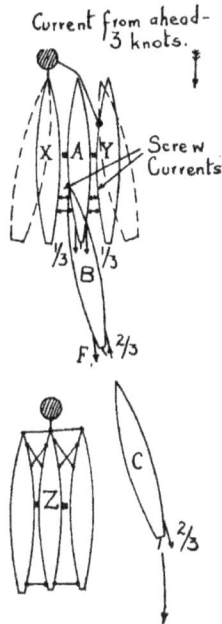

Fig. 10—Backing from between two destroyers with another group 100 yards astern

searchlight platforms of the other destroyers, it was necessary to start twisting the ship, so as to point it clear of the destroyer group astern. The port engine was backed full and starboard sent ahead standard. Rudder was put full right (B). The captain now must watch both bow and stern. Things are moving at a mile-a-minute clip and he must make a whole series of hair-trigger decisions—throw in unhesitatingly his last reserves of engine power and rudder angles. While his forecastle is grazing the side of a destroyer ahead, his stern is getting dangerously close to the destroyer group astern. The current is sweeping him down on to it and his twisting maneuver seems slow in taking effect. Judgment must be instantaneous as well as perfect. So must execution, both on the bridge and in the engine-rooms.

When finally pointed clear of the destroyer group astern (Z) the port engine was stopped, the starboard engine backed two-thirds, and the rudder put full left (C). When once clear, be duly thankful that the Lord was on your side. This is said in all seriousness, for I know of many dangers from which the ships on which I have served could not have escaped through human agency. A few words of earnest prayer have a most satisfactory and steadying effect before commencing a dangerous maneuver. At times the strongest man feels the need of a stronger power.

But now to our story again. Backing out from between two destroyers of a group alongside a tender presents no unusual features. The only difference is that the destroyer toward the tender will not be pushed off by the screw current. Thus, as you back out, the ship will pass somewhat closer to it than the destroyer on the outboard side. There will still, however, be ample room.

CHAPTER V

GOING AHEAD FROM ANOTHER DESTROYER

While usually it is safest to back away from alongside a destroyer, sometimes there are impelling reasons for going ahead. It may be necessary to avoid shoals or other vessels which are close astern. It is advantageous when only the outboard engine is ready for use. Also, it frequently will save some time and oil, but such considerations should never be decisive unless exceptionally favorable con-ditions reduce the inherent hazards of this method. It should not be attempted if there is insufficient wind or current to move the bow well out or if there is danger of the propellers fouling the anchor chain of the other ship or the buoy to which she is secured.

Let us take normal conditions with a good breeze or a weak current from ahead. When all is ready, take in the stern line, slack No. 2 and ease out the bow line gradually (Fig. 11). The ship will ride to No. 3 line and the wind or current will push the bow out slowly. The stern will remain in about the same position or come in slightly. Control the swing of the ship

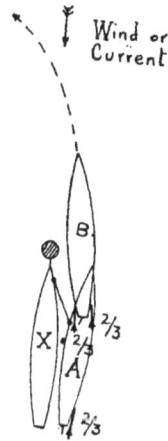

FIG. 11.—Going ahead from a de-stroyer.

by taking strains on the bow line from time to time. If there is current try to keep the ship parallel with some inboard rudder. Theoretically it should work, but practically it will have little effect. Have the officer in charge aft keep you informed of the distance between propeller guards. Do not let this get less than three feet. Usually the ship will take a position with about fifteen yards between bullnoses, one to two yards between your large fender and the other ship's side, and an equal distance between propeller guards. This is favorable for commencing the maneuver. Don't be in a hurry to begin. Wait until you get everything just right.

Put the rudder amidships. Go ahead two-thirds with the outboard engine. Cast off all the forecastle lines as the ship forges ahead (A). Do not use the inboard engine at first. There is a real danger that the propeller blades will hit the other ship. Also, it will suck the water from between the ships, with a consequent tendency to draw your stern in. Ordinarily your propeller guard will pass along the other ship's side at a distance of about one yard. Use inboard rudder as necessary to keep it this far away. When the ship has gone ahead about three-quarters of her length and the propeller guard is well clear— at least two yards—the inboard engine may be started ahead two-thirds. At the same time put the rudder full inboard to swing your stern out (B). Usually it is not necessary to use the inboard engine in this maneuver. Often, if there is any chance of your propeller fouling the anchor chain or buoy, it is highly undesirable to do so. This strong probability of being able to get away with the outboard engine only makes it preferable to go ahead rather than astern when the inboard engine is out of commission.

Sometimes in this maneuver your stern will be drawn in dangerously close soon after starting ahead—possibly because of a current eddy you have not been able to detect or a sudden yaw toward you of the other vessel. Put the rudder inboard 15 degrees; if necessary, increase it to 25 degrees. As a final measure go standard ahead with the outboard engine. Almost always this will swing your stern clear. But even if the propeller guard rubs the other ship's side a bit, no appreciable injury will result, provided always you refrain from using the inboard engine. Sometimes in a strong current the buoy to which the other vessel is secured will ride as much as ten yards from side to side. If it takes a yaw toward you as you start the maneuver, there will be a strong possibility of your propeller hitting it or its mooring chain. Such a situation occurred once at Charleston (Fig. 12). The maneuver was commenced as usual (*A*). The various measures above recommended to swing the stern clear were used, but did not have the required effect. As a last resort the inboard engine was backed two-thirds (*B*). This was effective immediately and the stern came out nicely. Before the buoy was reached the inboard engine was stopped again to avoid the possibility of fouling the mooring chain (*C*). The outboard engine was continued at standard ahead and the rudder kept at full left. A curving track across the bow of the other destroyer resulted. Such a track is usual in this maneuver, except when the current is very strong from ahead.

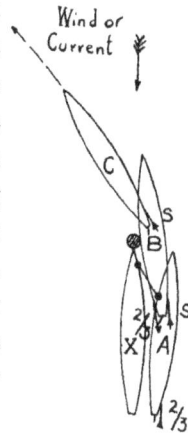

Fig. 12.—Alternate method when swept in too close.

In very rare cases, when there is a strong current, the ship will ride out from the other destroyer on No. 3 line, keeping almost parallel to her. Wait until you have about fifteen yards between the ships and then go ahead two-thirds with both engines. Although this expedient has been tried under all conditions, I can recall but one case where it worked. Theoretically, when riding to No. 3 line, the bow should point in. Actually it will insist on pointing out, and if you keep the bow line slack the propeller guards will come together. In destroyer handling facts, not theories, govern.

A particularly favorable situation for going out ahead occurs when your destroyer is the outboard one of several secured to a tender or oiler. Then there is no anchor chain or buoy to complicate the problem.

Chapter VI

LEAVING A TENDER OR OILER

Generally it is easier to back away from a large ship, such as an oiler or tender, than from another destroyer. Her sides are high and clear. A number of large fenders hold you off. The wedging-out effect of the inboard screw current is much greater, because of the nearly vertical form of the underwater hull and greater draft of the larger vessel. The effect lasts longer, because your propeller will not clear the larger vessel's stern until you have moved astern half a ship length.

When wind and current are at right angles, a large vessel will head more directly into the current than will a destroyer group. This is an advantage when you leave from the lee side. The dangerous pushing-on effect of the current, illustrated in Fig. 5, will be much reduced. On the other hand, when you leave from the weather side of the large vessel, the blowing-on effect of the wind will be a maximum—much more dangerous than in Fig. 6. However, in this case you can place much reliance on the strong effect of the screw current, which in most cases will more than counterbalance that of the wind. Backing two-thirds, instead of the usual one-third, is recommended.

It is not desirable to go ahead from immediately alongside a large vessel. Her bow extends far ahead and overhangs so as to catch your upper works and stays; also, her anchor chain makes a dangerous hazard, particularly when taut. When attempting this maneuver, try to get every possible favorable condition in your favor and wait until her anchor chain tends on the other bow. As a choice between two evils, the inboard engine may be used rather earlier than is desirable when going ahead from another destroyer.

Chapter VII

LEAVING A DOCK

There is a marked difference between leaving a dock and another ship. Where the dock has a solid side wall underwater your screw current has a very favorable effect, but when this current works against a few piles only its effect is negligible.

The effect of wind and current when leaving a dock usually is more unfavorable than when leaving a vessel at anchor or secured to a buoy. In the latter case, if there is either wind or current, the ship will ride to it and eliminate its effect. If there are both wind and current, the ship will ride to their resultant, and this will reduce their unfavorable effect materially. On the other hand, a ship leaving a dock may have either wind or current, or both, very unfavorable. Also, there may be wind or current eddies alongside docks which it will be difficult to detect.

To counterbalance these unfavorable conditions, your upper works are well above the level of the dock and it is seldom that there is anything they can foul. Also, you can work the ship along the dock with lines or engines—your wooden guard rail sliding along the piling and holding the ship off under the most unfavorable conditions of wind and current.

It is very rare that there is a chance to go ahead from alongside a dock. It is much better, when conditions permit, to back out. Under normal conditions, with no wind or current, this is a very simple operation.

When wind or current tends to carry the ship off the dock slack the lines so as to let the ship go out bodily for fifteen or twenty yards. Take slight strains on the appropriate lines to keep the ship parallel. When out the desired distance go ahead or astern with both engines, or twist the ship to point in the right direction. At Yorktown the face of the oil dock is parallel to the river bank (Fig. 13). Destroyer *A* was ordered to leave first. It was impossible to go directly ahead because of other vessels, *Y* and *Z*. There were shoals astern which made backing off somewhat risky. Fortunately the wind was from the inboard beam and blowing rather freshly. Its effect was reënforced by a current against the port bow. When lines were slacked the ship was carried out bodily by wind and current (*B*) until well clear of the destroyers ahead *Y* and *Z*. Then it was a simple matter to cast off lines and go ahead with both engines and a little outboard rudder. When wind or current are favorable make them work for you.

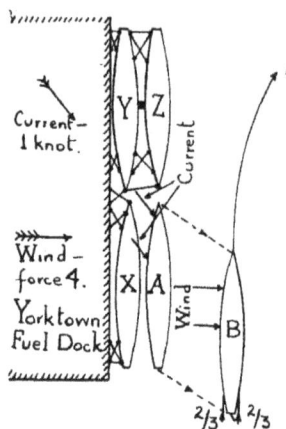

Fig. 13.—Leaving dock with favorable wind and current.

When wind or current, or both, are forcing you against the dock complications commence. First, assume that the dock has solid underwater side walls, as at the Naval Air Station, Pensacola, or the fueling station at Melville, R. I. Then you have the aid of a powerful screw current to counterbalance the wind or current effect. Let us take a simple case, which recently required solution at Pensacola (Fig. 14). A force-four breeze was blowing the ship directly on the dock. Here is your receipt: Heave the bow well in with the bow line on the capstan. Back two-thirds both engines and cast off the lines when the ship begins to move (*A*). The screw current just counteracted the wind effect, and no more. The guard rail kept just about six inches from the cross work of piling inlaid in the concrete as the ship

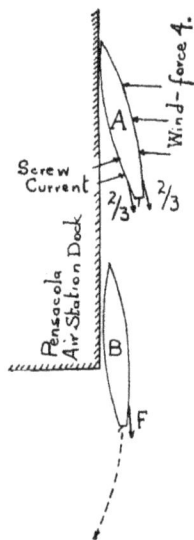

Fig. 14.—Leaving dock with unfavorable wind.

moved rapidly astern. It looked as if the overhang of our bow might scrape against the corner of the dock with possible injury to airports—and remember that those of the forward crew's compartment are only a few feet above the water line and constitute one of a destroyer's most vulnerable points. So it was decided to swing the bow out as soon as the stern was past the end of the dock and the effect of the screw current against it was lost. Therefore, when the stern was about thirty yards past the dock the inboard engine was stopped; the out-

board engine was backed full speed; and the rudder put hard inboard (*B*). The bow was swung out sharply and it easily cleared the dock.

Another vessel astern is a further complication. Take an actual situation along the oil dock at Melville, where again we had the advantage of a solid side wall. (See Fig. 15.) Heave in the bow with the bow line to the capstan until the ship takes about an angle of 30 degrees with the dock.

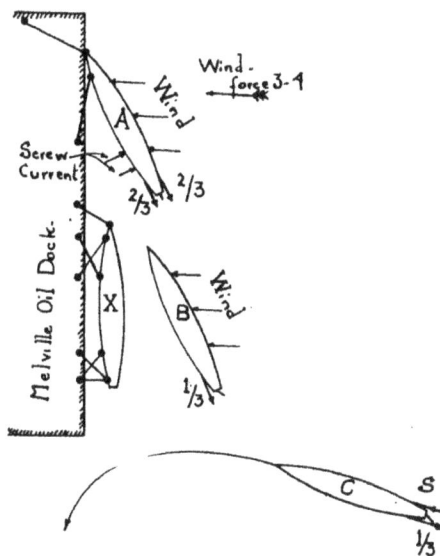

Fig. 15.—Leaving a dock with unfavorable wind and vessel astern.

Back out at two-thirds with both engines (*A*). In this case do not expect much effect from the inboard propeller, because it will be too far from the dock. But you will be pointed fair at the start of the maneuver and the tendency to back into the wind will help some. When clear of the ship astern *X*, stop the outboard engine and put the rudder full outboard (*B*). To save some steam reduce the backing speed of the inboard engine to one-third. You will now back rapidly into the wind. When sufficient maneuvering room has been gained go ahead standard with the outboard engine. When headway has been gained against the backing of the inboard engine, put the rudder full inboard (C). When swinging freely stop the inboard engine and turn clear of the end of the dock. Remember that no attempt has been made to draw our figures to scale or to use exactly the right turning circles.

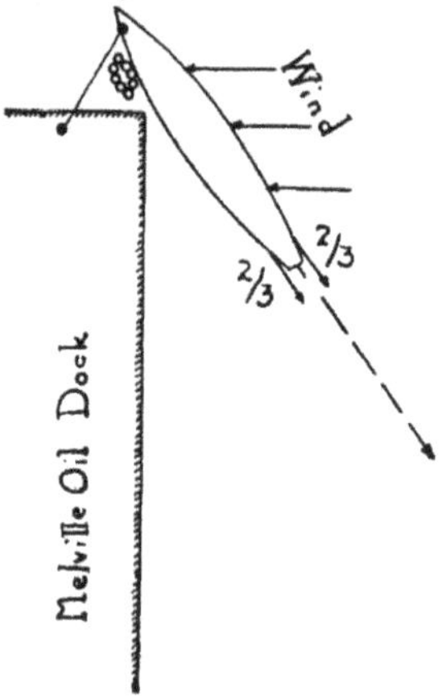

Assume now a similar, but more difficult, situation. The wind is stronger or perhaps a current is setting you on the dock. At any rate you cannot swing your stern out as in A, (Fig. 15). Haul the ship ahead until the stem projects thirty yards or so beyond the end of the dock (Fig. 16). Hold your No. 2 line and kick ahead the outboard engine. Twist the ship about the corner of the dock as a pivot until you have an angle of 30 degrees with its face. A group of piles about five yards off the end of the dock at Melville provides an excellent

FIG. 16.—Alternate method with unfavorable wind.

pivot for such a maneuver. Use your cylindrical rope fender between the piles and the forecastle to prevent airports from being cracked. When all set back off at two-thirds speed.

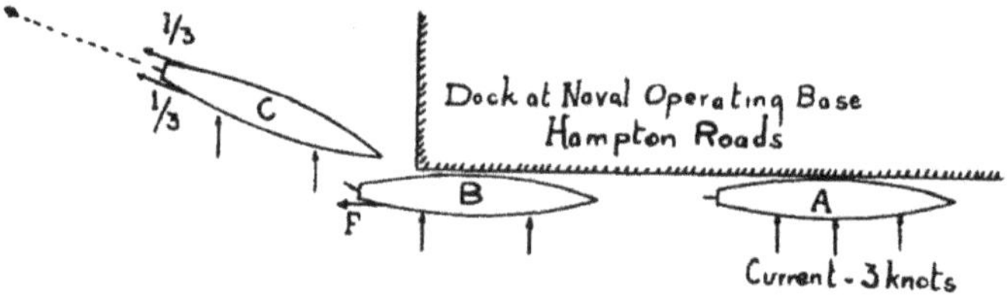

FIG. 17.—Leaving an open dock with unfavorable current.

Next assume a dock with no solid underwater side wall, such as at the Naval Operating Base, Hampton Roads. There the effect of the screw current will help you little or none. Take a destroyer at A in Fig. 17. A 3-knot current is pushing you against the dock. Work the ship slowly out along the dock with engines and lines. Let the guard rail, but not the propeller guard, rub against the piling. Get the stern about thirty yards beyond the dock with the propeller well clear (B). Then put the rudder full inboard, back the outboard engine full, and cast off lines quickly. This will swing the ship around the end of the dock and hold the bow out against the current. The decreasing beam of the destroyer at the bow will give a few yards more as a factor of safety. When clear of the dock (C) back away with both engines.

It might be asked how the problem would be solved if your ship A, had another vessel astern, secured to the dock near B. In such a case, I suggest that you ask for the services of an expert pilot—like those in the Norfolk navy yard—and two good tugs. Or better still, wait until the tide changes.

Now take another case which may require solution. You are secured to a long dock along, and parallel to, a river bank. There are ships ahead and astern with only a few yards clearance. We had such a problem at Mobile (Fig. 18). First, run

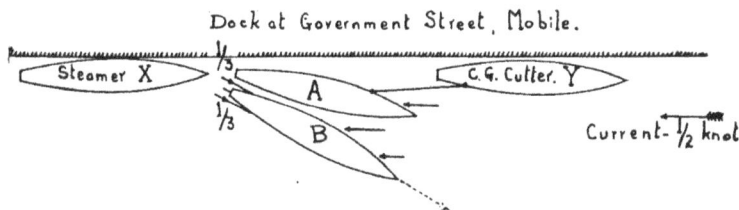

FIG. 18.—Leaving a dock between two other vessels, using a current from ahead.

a line from your inboard bow to the outboard quarter of the ship ahead (Y). By means of this line and some very cautious jockeying with the engines work the bow out clear (A). Take great care to keep the inboard propeller clear of the piles which support the dock. Obtain constant reports from the officer aft. If there is possibility of touching the piles, stop the engine immediately. In fact, it is safest to limit the use of the inboard engine to kicks of five to ten seconds, so as to keep the ship well in hand. If the propeller is not turning a slight contact with the piling will cause no damage. Never count upon the propeller guard keeping the propeller clear. It will cut through a rotten pile like a knife and let the wheel hit the underwater part. Then all you can do is to ask for a new propeller—and such requests are not received with enthusiasm.

Once your bow is clear of the ship ahead the current along the dock will gradually push it out farther until finally it is pointed clear. Then you can go ahead, remembering not to use the inboard propeller until it is well clear of the dock (B). Take plenty of time in a maneuver like this and use the engines with caution. Often when the problem seems insolvable, just stop everything and see what will happen. Sometimes your little ship will do just what you want her to—for no discoverable reason. Of course, this advice applies only when there is no way on the ship and no immediate danger impends.

On occasion it may be necessary to leave a dock without men to handle your lines. Usually it will be easy enough for one of your own men, a nimble seaman, to cast off the last line and jump aboard before the ship is clear. When you must make a quick get-away run the bight of a line around a bollard and use this for the last line to be thrown off.

CHAPTER VIII

MANEUVERING IN NARROW WATERS

First, assume that your ship is at anchor and pointed away from the entrance of the harbor. There is very limited room in which to turn. Here is a method of twisting the ship through 110 degrees without using the engines. When there is no current a destroyer anchored alone will yaw as much as 30 degrees from the direction of the wind (Fig. 19). Decide which end of the yaw will point you best for leaving the harbor. Have the anchor break ground when the ship is in position A. If in no hurry, remain stopped for a few minutes. The wind will blow your bow around until it comes from about 20 degrees abaft the beam. This is the normal position in which the ship will lie without way on. When you have been blown around enough, go ahead two-thirds with the appropriate engine and full rudder (B). This will swing you rapidly to your course, without having wasted a gallon of oil or churning the harbor into foam. Gonaives, Haiti, is an excellent place to practice this maneuver.

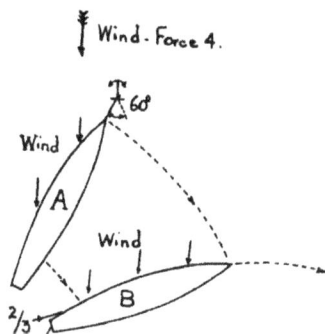

Fig. 19.—Getting under way and using the wind to point the ship.

If getting under way with a division, sneak up the anchor a few minutes before the signal, when you are at the proper limit of the yaw. When the signal is executed, the wind will have pointed you fair for leaving the harbor. In these days of economy and engineering competitions, the division commander should make no objection.

If there is not enough turning room ahead, but plenty astern, have the anchor, as before, break ground at the best end of the yaw (Fig. 20). Back the appropriate engine one-third for a few minutes with full rudder (*A*). The tendency to back into the wind will reën-force the turning effect of engine and rudder. The ship will swing very rap-idly. When you have turned enough or the stern is approaching shoal wa-ter, stop the engine, put the other ahead two-thirds,

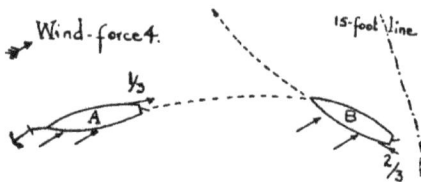

Fig. 20.—Getting under way and turning in the York River.

and shift the rudder when headway is gained (*B*). If this will not point you fair, repeat the process. Whenever possible have way on the ship when turning. Use one engine and full rudder to get the maximum turning effect. This is much more economical in fuel than to try to twist the ship on her heel with one engine going ahead and the other astern. Get into the habit of handling the ship with low engine powers. Then you always have the situation in hand, and you can use high powers with their full effect when demanded. To shift the subject rather suddenly: Remem-ber than you can use a leadsman aft as well as forward and that it is a very good thing to do so in narrow waters.

Consider now a turn prior to anchor-ing or landing alongside other vessels. When anchoring in a strong current it is advisable to be heading into it. This often will require a 180-degree turn. Take a comparatively wide turning area, as at Ninety-sixth Street, North

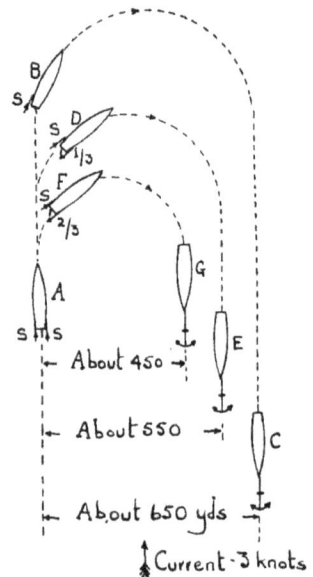

Fig. 21.—Turning in the North River to anchor against the current.

River (Fig. 21). To get good headway prior to turning go ahead standard speed both engines (*A*). Hug the bank, allowing a little room for your stern to come out when you begin to turn. Put the rudder over full as quickly as the helmsman can spin the wheel. Stop the inboard engine (B). This is the best and most economical method of turning in a fairly wide area. The ship will swing very rapidly, with a tactical diameter of about 650 yards (C). If the space is not so wide, the turning effect may be increased by backing the inboard engine one- or two-thirds $(D$ and $F)$. This, with your initial momentum, will still allow the ship the headway so necessary for a quick and economical turn. The ship will turn in from 550 to 450 yards $(E$ and G.)

Sometimes, due to restricted space or the effect of wind or current, it will not be possible to get around in one continuous turn. Take a typical situation at Charleston (Fig. 22). Two lines of destroyer groups are secured to mooring buoys planted along the edge of the shoal banks of the Cooper River. They are riding to a flood tidal current of three knots. A force-three breeze is blowing from the opposite direction.

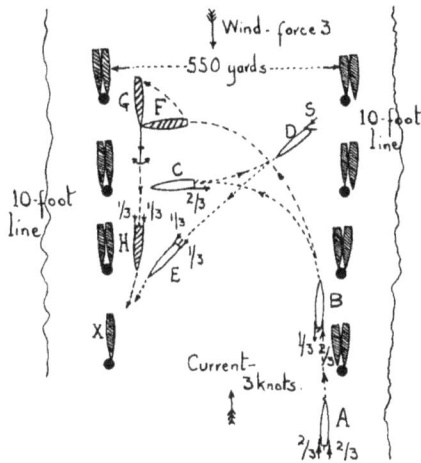

FIG. 22.—Turning in a restricted area with wind and current.

Speed is limited to two-thirds to avoid damage by the stern wave. It is required to go along the port side of destroyer X. Hug the right-hand line of destroyer groups at two-thirds speed and at a distance of fifty yards (A). When your stern clears the sterns of the vessels of the first group, spin the rudder full left and back the port engine one-third; continue the starboard engine ahead two-thirds (B). When nearing the left-hand line stop the starboard engine. Back the port engine two thirds. Shift the rudder to full right when sternway is gained (C).

The current will sweep the ship down bodily, but, as it is practically uniform in strength between the two destroyer lines, it
will have no effect upon the turn. There will be a distinct tendency to back into the wind and this will assist the turn. When
you have backed down as far as possible (*D*), stop the port engine. Send the starboard engine ahead standard. When
headway is gained shift the rudder to full left. This usually
will complete the turn. When pointed fair go ahead one-third
both engines for the landing (*E*).

If the wind were with the current, it would be more difficult
to effect the turn by this method. When you commenced
backing from position *C* the ship would probably go in a straight
line across the river instead of turning into position *D*. You
might charge back and forth across the river without turning
the ship at all, always being carried down by the current. It
will save time and oil in such a situation to swing round an
anchor. Remember your ship is over one hundred yards long
and be sure that your stern will clear all vessels and obstructions
while swinging. Therefore, turn the ship as far as possible
before anchoring. Use fifteen fathoms of chain—it makes no
difference if you drag a little (*F* and *G*). After swinging to the
current (*G*) weigh the anchor and proceed at one-third speed to
the landing (*H*). Incidentally, you should use the port anchor.
Then the chain will not grate across the stem while you are
swinging. Also, after heaving it up, you can let it hang over
the side until after completing the landing. On one occasion I
saw a landing made with the inboard anchor hanging over the
bow and its fluke punched a dent into the side of the other ship.

Perhaps readers may wonder why we did not commence the
turn from a position outside the right line of destroyers. This
would have made it necessary to start the turn through an
interval of open water only about one hundred yards wide. Due
to the shoal water it would be necessary to hug the port side of
the first destroyer group. It is rather doubtful whether your
turning circle would clear the second group, particularly as a
3-knot current would be carrying you toward it. This is an

entirely different proposition from that of passing through the
interval at right angles. It would require almost perfect judgment for success and failure would mean a veritable disaster.
We think it is not justified. The advantage gained by success
would not be worth the possible consequences of failure. A
destroyer captain in the course of years finds himself confronted
with hundreds of difficult situations. He must bear in mind
those old laws of probability and
chance, and always get as many
chances as he can in his favor. He
must give important weight to the
probable results of a poor, as well
as a good, maneuver. A failure
which results only in loss of fuel
and prestige manifestly has advantages over one which may
cause important damage and lead
to a court-martial.

If the space available for turning
is 250 yards or less, it is well to
twist the ship without appreciable
fore-and-aft motion, despite the
waste of oil which this entails. In
such cases it is essential to take
every advantage offered by the
current to assist the engines in
turning the ship. The usual
method is to place the bow or

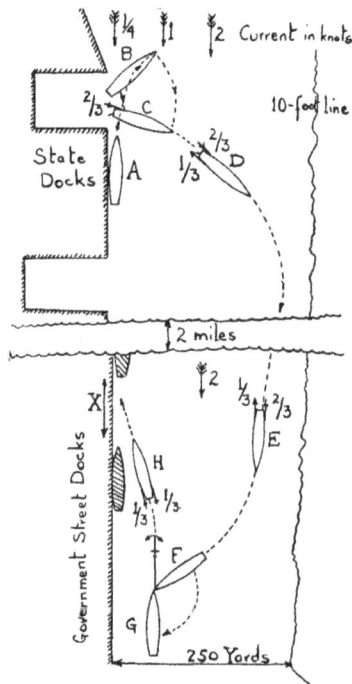

Fig. 23.—Turning in Mobile
Harbor with and against a current.

stern, as may be appropriate, in the center of the channel,
where the current is strongest, keeping the other end close to
the bank, where the current is weaker or even slack. Fig. 23
shows a typical case. Destroyer A was pointed upstream alongside the State Docks at Mobile. It was cautiously worked ahead
under very low power and the bow pointed out into the river (B).
Here the bow was in a strong ebbing current, while the stern
was in virtually slack water. With the engines stopped, the

current carried the bow through an angle of 70 degrees into position C. Then the rudder was put full right and the port engine sent ahead two-thirds. A kick astern of the starboard engine quickly pointed the ship down the river (D).

It was necessary to go alongside the dock at Government Street. A space X about 110 yards long had been reserved for us, between two other ships. It had been planned originally to make the landing with the current, so we would be pointed right when we finally left port. But this current proved much stronger than we had expected—so strong, in fact, as to make the landing extremely difficult and even dangerous. It was deemed advisable, after one most ineffective attempt, to turn the ship through 180 degrees and approach the dock against the current.

We hugged the right bank as closely as we dared. In position E the rudder was placed full right and we tried to twist the ship with the engines—two-thirds ahead port and one-third astern starboard. We soon discovered that the turn was going to prove very difficult, for the current which had assisted us in the first turn was fighting us in the second. As the bow got out toward the center of the stream the swing stopped. The last resort was to swing around an anchor. It should have been let go near the left bank (F). Then, after the ship had swung into the current (G), it would have been a simple matter to have weighed anchor and headed toward the landing (H). Actually we let go about in the center of the river and eased to fifteen fathoms. As we started to swing around the anchor, it was seen that our stern would come close to several small craft anchored off the right bank. To avoid them the chain was quickly veered to ninety fathoms and the starboard engine kicked ahead. After completing the turn the anchor was gotten up and the landing made. This experience taught a very forceful lesson: never to anchor where there is not ample room to swing.

A continuation of this situation—and another turn—is shown in Fig. 24. With lines and engines, as in Fig. 18, swing the bow out clear of the ship ahead and into the center of the river (B). There it will be swept down rapidly by the strong current. The stern, near the dock, will also be carried down, but much more slowly, unless the current effect is counteracted by the engines. To do this keep the port engine going ahead two-thirds and the starboard engine alternating between one- or two-thirds astern, keeping fore-and-aft motion off the ship (B). This will hold the stern in practically the same position, while the bow is swept gradually through an arc downstream. When the ship has been twisted enough, go ahead with the port engine standard speed with full right rudder

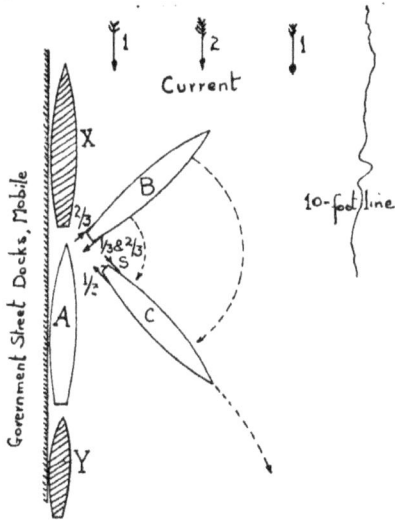

FIG. 24.—Turning with aid of current and from between two ships in Mobile Harbor.

(C). Back the starboard engine for a time to accelerate the swing. Sometimes a powerful eddy will turn the ship if it is placed in

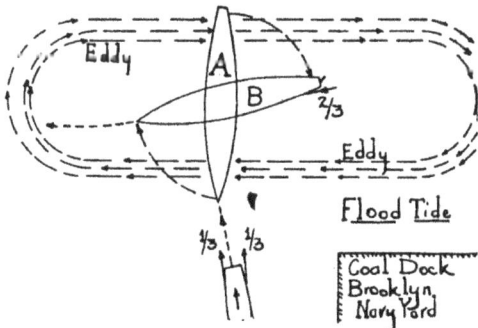

FIG. 25.—Using an eddy in the East River to twist the ship.

the proper position. Such an eddy waits to serve you just outside the Navy Yard at Brooklyn if you know where to place your ship—or to fight you if you don't. When there is flood tide in the East River there is a strong countercurrent past the edge of the fuel dock (Fig. 25). Therefore, back slowly out into the river and place the ship with her bow just outside the line of docks (A).

The outer part of the eddy ellipse will carry the stern upstream, while the inner carries the bow downstream. In a few minutes the ship will be twisted through 90 degrees and pointed downstream along the eastern bank (B). Then go ahead two-thirds with the port engine and right rudder.

When ebb tide is running the eddy is reversed, but equally at your service (Fig. 26). Back out and take the same position (A). Now the outer half of the eddy will carry the stern downstream, while the inner half swings the bow upstream. The ship will be revolved quickly through 225 degrees and pointed fair down the western bank (B). You can expedite the last 45 degrees by going ahead two-thirds on the starboard engine with left rudder. Don't try to fight the eddy—let it work for you. Its power isn't charged against your engineering performance. It will turn you through 225 degrees much quicker than you can turn 90 degrees against it with full engine power.

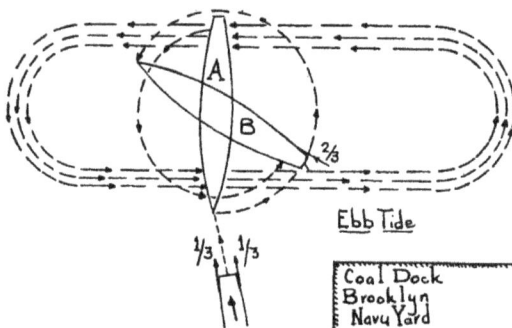

Fig. 26.—Using an eddy in the East River to twist the ship.

For a really interesting quarter of an hour just try to turn a destroyer opposite the Astor House Hotel at Shanghai. The river makes a sharp bend there and you find a gap in the line of mooring buoys which runs along the center of the river. On the farther side a bank of shoals extends well out; numerous Chinese craft at anchor mark its limits. You might as well decide to use full twisting power from the very start—to get the job done as quickly as possible. As your propellers churn the muddy waters, whole fleets of clumsy sailing junks and slowly sculled freight sampans nonchalantly insist on grazing your stem and stern. As all these craft are virtually out of control in the strong 3-knot current it is best to keep fore-and-aft motion off the ship after you get started around. But, better still, don't try to turn at all in such a place. Go up the river a mile past the mooring buoys and dense traffic and swing round an anchor. Very often in this game you will find that the longest way round is the shortest way home.

Often, when it is necessary to turn in restricted waters, more maneuvering room can be gained by backing down half a mile or so. Key West is a good illustration. Destroyer A was secured along the coal dock X at the Naval Station. A line of shoals, YZ, narrowed the channel—traced very roughly in Fig. 27. The ship was backed down at one-third speed until her stern was opposite the end of the shoal Z. Then the port engine was stopped, the backing speed of the starboard engine increased to two-thirds and the rudder put full left (B). After getting well out into the wider area (C) the remainder of the turn was completed in the usual manner.

There are many situations where it will be necessary to go astern for considerable distances. Leaving the oil dock at Guantanamo is a familiar example. Destroyers handle and steer very well when going astern, except when a strong breeze is blowing. Then the tendency to back into the wind introduces a fairly serious complication. For example, take a force-five breeze on the port beam. To hold a steady course it will be necessary to stop the starboard engine and put the rudder well right. Under these conditions it is almost impossible to swing your stern away from the wind and your control over the ship is very limited.

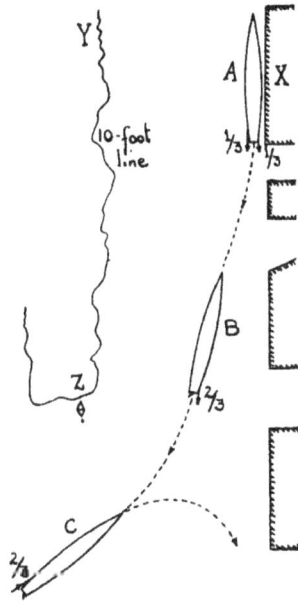

FIG. 27.—Backing away from the dock at Key West.

Often two destroyers will be lying together to an anchor or buoy with orders to get under way, turn, and leave port. If the area is restricted, but clear of obstructions, and without a strong current it will frequently be a good plan to get under way and make the turn together rather than singly (Fig. 27A). See that all the mooring lines are taut and the strain distributed equally among their parts. For a turn to port both ships put their rudders full left; the right ship *A* goes ahead two-thirds starboard engine; the left ship *B* backs one-third port engine. As you have now about forty-five feet between the two propellers in use, as against about fifteen feet for a single destroyer, the turning diameter is very small, probably about two hundred yards. The turn is made quickly and with little fuel expenditure. When the ships are pointed toward the entrance, stop all engines and steady them with the rudders (*C* and *D*). One then backs away slowly (*E*) into second position in formation, and you are ready to proceed. New London is a good place to try out this maneuver. We used it here with excellent effect.

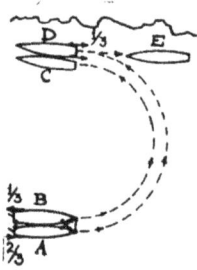

Fig. 27A.—Turning a destroyer group together.

Accurate steering is essential when proceeding through thick traffic or narrow and intricate channels, particularly when strong currents are running. To steer properly the ship must have a correct trim. This is either an even keel or a little down by the stern. A destroyer down by the head answers the rudder very sluggishly. It takes a long time to get her swinging, and even longer to check the swing. Before entering dense traffic, such as will be found in the North and East Rivers at New York or in the Wangpoo at Shanghai, appoint a quartermaster to keep a lookout on each side. They should report all ships leaving docks or approaching and all whistle signals, including those made to other ships as well as yours.

Unless there is reason to the contrary, keep well out toward the center of the harbor when there is much cross traffic, as in the North River. This reduces the effect of your wake on docks and vessels secured to them. It permits changes of course to either side and gives much more room for maneuvering. It prevents your being surprised by tugs and ferryboats shooting out from the docks. Of course, in the entrance to a harbor, where there is no cross traffic, it is well to hug the right edge of the channel.

Consider every ship close at hand in your running estimate of the situation. Some vessels may be a direct menace. Others which cannot collide with you may force ships, which otherwise would have passed well clear, toward your projected line of advance. Such vessels might be called an indirect menace. In very thick traffic give one or two ships your primary attention, but don't leave the others entirely out of the picture. Usually it is not the obvious danger which catches you in her toils, for all your attention is concentrated on it. It is a more distant and less apparent danger, which you hastily dismiss from consideration, that is really dangerous. This principle has a perfect illustration in running a destroyer through traffic. As you cannot give full attention to more than two or three ships at the most, and sometimes to one only, appoint one or more officers to watch other ships, as pointed out from time to time. This is particularly desirable when there are a number of ships close astern.

Usually it is best to avoid whistle signals, and in particular when there are several vessels to which the signal might apply. If collision is possible with a certain ship, indicate your intentions early by a change of course which will show her unmistakably which side you desire to pass. The other captain will usually disclose his intentions in a similar manner. Often you can run up through all the traffic in the North River without touching the whistle. If, however, you have clearly disclosed your intentions and the other vessel does not point clear, give a signal quickly and insist upon the correct answer. Repeat your signal until you get it, or enliven the occasion with a danger signal. In passing on opposite courses do not blow two blasts unless its is perfectly apparent that this is the only side you can pass without danger. Watch out for a situation where the other ship is one point on your starboard bow and heading at your stem. This is the most dangerous set-up you can meet. Give right rudder early in the game, and follow it quickly with one blast if the other ship does not point clear. Stop engines if necessary. It is nice to say that you have run up the North River at fifteen knots without once touching the annunciator; but don't let the desire to pull off a grandstand play lead you to run unnecessary risks of real disaster.

While you have a clear lane ahead, get through as quickly as possible, using the highest speed permitted by harbor regulations. But never forget that your stern wave may cause much damage; or it will sound like a lot when the claims are made. Watch your wave carefully when passing dredges, barges with low freeboard, sailing yachts, and piers or bridges under construction. It is often an excellent procedure to enter in the log that you slowed to one-third speed when passing such craft or work. These injunctions as to speed apply particularly when passing through the Cape Cod Canal or other very narrow channels.

It is dangerous to pass another vessel going in the same direction in a narrow canal. It is quite a feat to pass a 40-foot yacht in the Cape Cod Canal, because at eight knots it will take you several minutes to get past and you must be careful not to swing your stern toward her. One of the thrills of a lifetime was to hold my breath when the *Peary* passed the *Black Hawk* in the Suez Canal. The latter was making about twelve knots and the *Peary* ran past us at twenty. We could have thrown a biscuit across. It was a superb maneuver—one of those *beau gestes* that every real destroyer captain loves to make. But once is enough!

Avoiding traffic in a dense fog in a harbor, say Boston, is an interesting experience. Very slow speed and frequent fog signals are the essentials. Five knots is quite fast enough. When you hear a whistle ahead or on the bow, stop, blow two long blasts, and coast along until the situation clears. Maneuvering signals on the whistle are of little value in a dense fog. They must not be made until the other ship can be seen, and then it is too late to do much. Send a quartermaster aloft; he may be able to see over the top of the fog bank. Put a good man in the eyes of the ship to listen for buoys—it is difficult to hear them on the bridge through the roar of the blower.

To go through a narrow passage, such as Pollock Rip Slue, in a dense fog is rather a different problem. Here the traffic does not present much difficulty, as only the steamers making the regular run will pass through in a dense fog. Very dangerous shoals and a strong treacherous current are the principal enemy forces in your estimate of the situation. Through much of the passage the current runs at a large angle with the channel. This makes it desirable to go as fast as ten or twelve knots, heading 5 to 10 degrees from the true course to allow for the lateral component of the current. Put several good men in the eyes of the ship to listen for the bell and whistle buoys. Our chief boatswain's mate appointed himself to this duty and always heard the buoys before we could on the bridge. Pass close to all lightships to get in the exact center of the channel and to observe the force and direction of the current. In making such a passage in clear weather it is good practice to assume a fog and act accordingly—then see how you come out. Write down the results for reference when you go through on a later occasion and find that Old Man Fog is there to greet you with his clammy grip.

Often strong eddies or even whirlpools will be encountered in a swiftly running river. They occur usually where there are sharp bends, shoals, or islands. In the Yangtze these whirlpools are known as "chow water." They have been capitalized largely by the various Chinese religious orders, which have dotted the banks nearby with conspicuous "joss-houses." There the poor junkmen are supposed to propitiate the river gods, or perhaps dragons, with liberal financial offerings—not by any means to the disadvantage of their priests. But chow water which struck terror into the heart of the skipper of a slow, clumsy sailing junk has slight effect upon a powerful destroyer. I refer, of course, to the lower part of the river practicable for that type. I remember the elaborate precautions we took before entering our first stretch of chow water in Silver Island Pass; but in a few days we let the regular helmsman keep the wheel and went through as a matter of course. As the bow hits the first sector of the swirl it is carried rapidly to one side. Then it reaches the second part of the eddy and is swept back in the opposite direction, a movement which is reënforced by the pressure of the first part against your stern. The natural tendency is to put on full rudder to counteract the first effect of the eddy against your bow, so that when you get into the opposite effect, you are caught with the rudder hard over in the wrong direction. Before you can get it off you will find yourself swinging much faster in the second direction than you were the first. We had this same experience recently in passing close to the eastern side of Hell Gate, when entering from the southward, and had to do some quick maneuvering with the engines. Therefore it is best to keep the rudder nearly amidships and run through at high speed, as much as twenty knots in bursts. The course will be a snake's track, but its general direction will be very close to the one you planned to steer. If you have an expert helmsman, well experienced in such work, he can keep your track from looking quite so much like a sine curve by watching the water ahead and having his rudder set in the right angle before the stem enters the swirl. Even then it is best to use not over 10 degrees of rudder.

Occasionally you will have trouble in making a turn around a sharp bend in a river against a strong current. The bow first projects beyond the bend and is caught by the full force of the current, which has not yet adjusted its direction to the bend in the river. The stern is out of the full strength of the current or may be in a counter current or eddy. The ship, in consequence, refuses to turn, even with full rudder. Such a situation occurred when standing out of the Navy Yard, Portsmouth, N. H., at fifteen knots (Fig. 27B). It developed with startling rapidity. Rudder was put full left and the port engine stopped (*A*). It was then backed one-third, two-thirds, and full in quick succession. While this started the swing, it was evident that the ship would not turn sharply enough to clear the right bank. It was necessary to kill her headway and at the same time continue the swing. This double purpose was accomplished by stopping the starboard engine (*B*). The port engine, which was kept backing full, forced the stern around and brought the ship to a stop. When the ship was pointed nearly fair (*C*), the port engine was stopped and the starboard engine sent ahead two-thirds. This soon brought the ship into the channel and pointed clear of the buoy (*D*). Such unexpected high-power maneuvering as this tests the engineering personnel most rigorously and shows

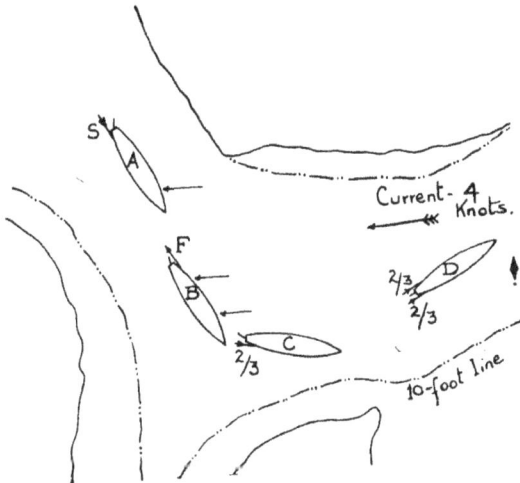

Fig. 27B.—Making a sharp turn in a river against a strong current below Portsmouth, N.H. (Enlarged from *Y*, Fig. 51.)

that they must be prepared at all times to execute any order from the bridge on the instant.

In getting under way from a harbor in which there are many small native boats, it is well to see that all are clear of your stern—for this is a good opportunity to pass a bottle of rum through one of the after air ports or maybe to steal a blanket. Once we had proceeded a few hundred yards from our anchorage in Gonaives when it was reported that a Haitian was sitting on our port propeller guard. It seems that his boat had been slightly forward of the guard when the ship moved ahead slowly. Before he realized what was happening, the guard had knocked him off his balance. Not being able to swim he had clutched it with a death grip and pulled himself to safety. As we stopped his companions rowed up frantically and rescued the adventurer from his predicament. Doubtless when the investigation of Haiti begins we will find this incident recorded as an American atrocity—not to mention some effective marksmanship with Very pistols and fire hose when such defensive measures seemed essential.

CHAPTER IX

CRUISING IN FORMATION

For engineering economy it is desirable while making long cruises to keep the main engine speeds as steady as possible. If variations from the standard speed do not exceed three revolutions the engineering set-up may be maintained without change, except for a slight adjustment of the throttle and the occasional cutting in or out of a burner.

To facilitate the maintenance of steady speeds the senior officer may indicate that exact station keeping is unnecessary. He may prescribe double distance or column open order. The latter formation is preferable. It permits a vessel to range from two hundred yards ahead to an equal distance behind her normal position without interfering with other vessels. It facilitates steering by keeping out of the wake of the ship ahead. And it allows stadimeter distances to be taken directly on the division leader and other vessels ahead. Distance should be kept on the division leader, rear ships using the small range finder mounted on the pelorus stand. Changes of revolutions should be made by ones or twos instead of fives. Division leaders in standard formation should adjust their position by changes of one revolution. The squadron leader must maintain an absolutely steady speed, using, if necessary, an extra man in the forward engine-room continually to check the revolutions. Helmsmen should steer compass courses, altered a degree or two by the officer of the deck as necessary. These methods of maintaining approximate station with maximum fuel economy would be essential in war-time cruises overseas and should be practiced frequently. During a recent long cruise our ship was in fifth position in the right column of a standard formation. On several occasions over nine hours passed without a change in revolutions. In tactical exercises, entrance into and departure from port, and other occasions where a show of efficiency is required exact station should be kept.

Column open order has many advantages in a fog. Close distance is then necessary to maintain contact. It is desirable to keep pointed clear of the ship ahead in case she suddenly stops. This last advantage was demonstrated on my first destroyer cruise. We were third ship in column proceeding at ten knots through a dense fog. The night before course had been set for Mt. Desert Rock, off the Maine coast. The course proved inconceivably accurate—so much so that about 0700 the next day the leading vessel sighted the rock about one hundred yards dead ahead. It was a landfall in the fullest sense of the word. The leader of course backed—we did not distinguish her three short blasts. The second ship also backed full speed—her whistle was out of commission. We missed her, but not by much. After that I have never followed directly in the wake of another ship in a dense fog. It has been found excellent practice to keep about 25 yards to one side with 150 yards distance between foremasts.

The use of position buoys by destroyers is unnecessary and highly undesirable. Much of your attention is focused, most uselessly, in trying to avoid the buoys. A searchlight should be pointed at the ship next astern, but only when it is too thick to see that ship. Much electricity and effort is wasted in this way.

When in normal column and on a steady course direct the helmsman to follow the leading ship without reference to intervening vessels. This is particularly effective in bad weather or in a following sea, which makes steering very erratic. Practically all helmsmen move the wheel about three times as much as is necessary. This constant swinging of the ship to and fro holds it back, as also does the inclined surface of the rudder. Much steam is wasted in the steering engine and there is more wear and tear on all the steering apparatus. Under normal conditions, with calm and deep water a range of 6 degrees of rudder is ample for a good helmsman to keep within

2 degrees of his course. An expert helmsman can do so with less. One of the clearest recollections of a midshipman's practice cruise are the exhortations of an old chief quartermaster named Boylan to use small rudder angles and not to move the wheel so much. This old fellow had been blown up in the *Maine* and is still after all these years a hero to me.

I never realized how good a helmsman could be until a Chinese pilot steered the *John D. Ford* from Nanking to Shanghai for ten straight hours, eating his meals, smoking cigarettes, walking about the bridge, and finally sitting easily on a high stool at the wheel. When that fellow moved the wheel a spoke it was an event. He wasn't a helmsman—but a magician. He had some sort of a spell over our little ship.

A destroyer captain should be a first-class helmsman himself. To keep in good practice he should take the wheel daily. If a helmsman should be doing poorly, it is well to take the wheel yourself for a few minutes to see if you can do better. If you can't, nothing need be said and you have avoided an injustice. If you can, the helmsman will see for himself. Again nothing need be said—if you can resist the temptation.

When the water shoals to about twenty-five feet steering becomes quite difficult. Often 15 degrees of rudder will be necessary to get the ship swinging. In entering the long channel leading up through Mobile Bay we found a most remarkable effect, which was repeated exactly at a passage a year later. Steering conditions were so queer that the best helmsman was put at the wheel. For over five minutes he used an *average* of 20 degrees left rudder to keep the ship on a steady course. This was at the exact spot where occurred the famous grapple between Farragut and the *Tennessee*. Perhaps this queer condition was responsible for that collision between the *Lackawanna* and *Hartford* which caused the admiral's famous signal to the former: "For God's sake get out of our way and anchor."

Keep the wheel working freely, the ropes well covered with graphite, and the sheaves well greased. The wheel ropes should be adjusted to the proper tension—not so tight as to make the wheel turn stiffly nor so loose as to let them ride over the edges of the sheaves. When going from a warm to a cold climate the ropes will contract and tighten up. Conversely, when going from cold into warm weather, the ropes become so slack that they may jump the sheaves. It is a simple matter to steer by hand for a few minutes and adjust the ropes to the proper tension. It is a wise precaution to have each helmsman coming on watch inspect the entire length of the ropes before relieving.

Keep the gyro repeaters in the steering engine-room and on the after steering station running. That is the only way to maintain them in good condition. To steer effectively from aft, either by hand or steam, it is essential that these repeaters be running at the time of the casualty. Weekly drills in steering from the after steering station and the steering engine-room should be routine. The captain should give the business of steering his personal attention.

To avoid the use of unnecessary blowers or too high a reserve of steam the division commander should keep the signal for full speed flying five minutes before execution. He should ordinarily indicate other changes in the speed of the guide by flag signals.

It is essential that the engine-room receive immediate and accurate information of prospective changes in the standard speed. It is dangerous to trust to a voice tube or telephone for such orders. After several misunderstandings we adopted the practice of sending a typewritten form to the engine-room by messenger—with the new standard speed entered in pencil by the officer of the deck. The wording of this form was: "When annunciators are rung three times the standard speed will be —— knots." When the messenger has reported delivery of the message and it is desired to execute the change, the annunciators are moved back and forth three times and stopped on any desired sector. The engine-room then makes the new standard speed or fraction thereof thus indicated. This has been found entirely satisfactory.

It is a good idea for the executive officer to take the morning watch under way when cruising and for the captain to hold down the bridge during the forenoon and afternoon watches—with a relief for lunch. This allows the other officers to attend to their ship's work. It permits the relief of both the engineer and his assistant from all deck watches. It lets the captain and executive keep their hand in. When conducting daily operations from a base it is well for the captain to keep the deck all the time the ship is under way—with relief for meals.

A steering light on the jack staff will prove a great convenience on a dark night. Punch a hole in a small tin can and fit it over the bulb of the anchor light with the hole aft. Such a light is useful also during high-speed maneuvers without lights. The hole should be so small as to show a mere dot of light which has no blinding effect.

CHAPTER X

HIGH-SPEED MANEUVERING

When maneuvering at twenty-seven knots it is desirable to have on board between 85,000 and 45,000 gallons of oil. If you have more, the forecastle may be submerged during a turn by the stern wave of the ship ahead. This will put the forecastle gun out of action, temporarily at least, and blind the people on the bridge by a curtain of spray. If you have less than 45,000 gallons the same stern wave may cause very heavy and prolonged lists. The *Toucey* entered a division practice with about 20,000 gallons of oil. During the approach at twenty-seven knots the ship ahead fell much behind her position. To counterbalance this we kept at about two hundred yards distance from her. During a right-angle turn we were caught in her stern wave. The ship listed 52 degrees and stayed there for fifteen seconds. The port propeller came half out of water and lifted a fountain of spray thirty feet in the air. Torch pots in the torpedo tubes were ignited and green seas cascaded into the engine-rooms. Fortunately the ammunition had not been taken from the racks and the tubes still were trained in. This incident demonstrated conclusively the danger of maneuvering at high speeds in formation in a very light condition.

Regardless of the amount of fuel on board it is well to get the bow up as much as possible before high-speed maneuvering, firing the forecastle gun in choppy water, or steaming into a rough sea. When making a full-power run alone in a calm sea, trim down about eighteen inches by the bow before speeding up. This will help to counteract the tendency of the stern to "squat" at high speeds and when you reach full power the ship will be fairly close to an even trim. When running full power it is best to have at least thirty fathoms of water. However, if necessary, the speed can be made in much less. We have run full power in Chesapeake Bay, where the water decreased at times to five fathoms. At high speeds a long swell from abaft the beam will cause the ship to roll deeply and hang at the end of the roll. A skillful helmsman can partly kill these rolls with the rudder, but at the expense of an erratic course. It is best to bring the sea about broad on the bow. This eliminates the roll and allows the spray to blow clear. That becomes very important in cold weather. Once at about 26 degrees the spray froze over the bridge windows to a thickness of several inches. The situation was much improved by changing course enough to let the spray blow over the side.

It is bad practice to change the standard speed during high-speed maneuvering. It is even more confusing to hoist that bewildering signal: "Steam at —— speed." With our present tactical methods it is necessary to use flank speed in battle. Unfortunately there is no method of indicating it to the engine-room with the annunciators without the possibility of mis-understanding. Five rings on the bell pulls is recommended; but care must be taken to pull them all the way up or the gongs will not ring below. Hoisting two speed pennants for flank speed is very unsatisfactory. The use of the speed pennant half-mast for full and two-blocks for flank speed is a possible solution.

A distance of 275 yards by stadimeter is very satisfactory for high-speed work. The wave effect of the ship ahead will hold you in this position despite a change of twenty or thirty revolutions. Thus, at this distance, you eliminate all difficulties of station keeping, except of course during a poor turn. Once second position in Division 43 was maintained at 275 yards for three hours of 27-knot maneuvering without changing a revolution. This distance is particularly useful for a destroyer which, due to a foul bottom or engineering deficiencies, is able to make little more than twenty-seven knots through the water.

When your distance is less than 275 yards at the beginning of a turn be careful not to get inside the wake of the ship ahead. The stern wave of a destroyer turning is exceptionally large on the inside of a turn. If your bow gets as much as twenty-five yards inside the wake, it will plow into the stern wave—the results you know already. The stern wave on the outside of the turn is much smaller. If you follow close in the track of the ship ahead during the turn, the stern wave will be altogether avoided and the ship will be very steady, with a moderate outboard list. When at distances over 275 yards the effect of the stern wave is much reduced and it is permissible to turn inside to gain distance. When taking station in rear of a destroyer making high speed on a steady course cut through her stern wave at rather a sharp angle and not too close to her stern. The effect of a light cruiser's stern wave at thirty knots is very similar to that of a destroyer's, and no greater.

At the beginning of a turn, during which it is desired to maintain the present distance, order "right (or left) rudder" at the normal point with reference to the wake of the ship ahead. The helmsman knows that this means "standard rudder," usually 22 degrees. Identify the wake of the leading ship and try to keep your bow a few yards inside it. You can then make the fine adjustments at the end of the turn by easing the rudder instead of increasing it. Pay no attention to the ship immediately ahead, if she makes a poor turn, except to avoid collision or her stern wave. If you follow her, you make an equally poor turn and embarrass the ships behind you. Alter the rudder angle during the turn between 15 and 28 degrees—the latter is enough to use except in emergency. When the ship has swung to within 15 degrees of the new course, order "rudder amidships." The helmsman uses his judgment as to how fast he turns the wheel to execute this order, depending upon the speed and other conditions. When pointed about right, give the order "follow," which indicates that the helmsman is to follow the leading ship. He does the rest.

If line of bearing formation is to be assumed give the helmsman the new course immediately after right (or left) rudder is ordered. In this case the rudder angle and the new course may be modified by a few degrees, depending upon whether you

were ahead of, or behind, station when the maneuver was commenced.   When 15 degrees from the course order "rudder
amidships, course ———." The helmsman knows the new course
from the beginning of the maneuver; if he does not get the order
to put the rudder amidships at the proper time he immediately
calls the captain's attention to this apparent omission. Early
service in submarines proved to me the necessity of having
cross checks on every important operation.   It is well to en-
courage all hands on the bridge to speak up quickly whenever
they think a mistake is being made.

Gaining distance on a turn is
an art in itself, and one of frequent
application. Unfortunately this is
done so much by the "seaman's
eye" that it is rather difficult to
describe its methods on paper.
However, let us try.

In high-speed maneuvering there
are many occasions when a ship
will get far behind its proper station.   The acceleration from five
to twenty-seven knots requires
many minutes—it used to be
twelve for Squantum destroyers.
During this period it is very difficult to maintain station.   After
the acceleration is completed the
division commander should, if
practicable, make several right-

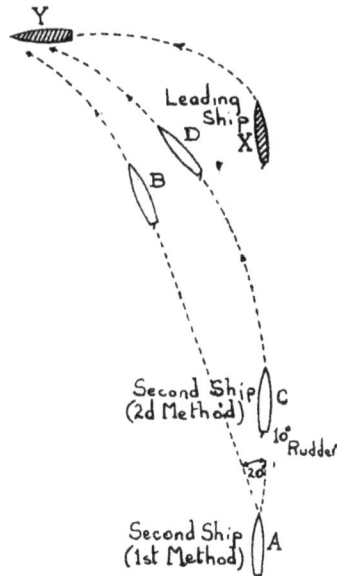

FIG. 28.—Gaining distance on a turn.

angle turns in order to give his ships a chance to rectify their
positions.

Several methods are available.   In Fig. 28 the first method
is applicable when you are 200 yards or more behind position.
When the leading ship X commences the turn you, in the second
ship, change course immediately 15 to 25 degrees toward him (A).
When about 250 yards from the leader's new track (B), put the

rudder over and take correct station behind him. Once at the beginning of a gunnery run the second ship dropped 1,050 yards behind the leader—each claimed to have made the acceleration correctly. After the first 90-degree change of course was completed the second ship was exactly in the desired station— distance 275 yards.

The second method is useful for gaining between one and two hundred yards. Well before reaching the normal turning point the second ship puts the rudder over 10 degrees (C). It makes a continuous and very wide turn with about that rudder (D). This reduces the distance to be run and avoids the retardation which the leader experiences through the use of a large rudder angle.

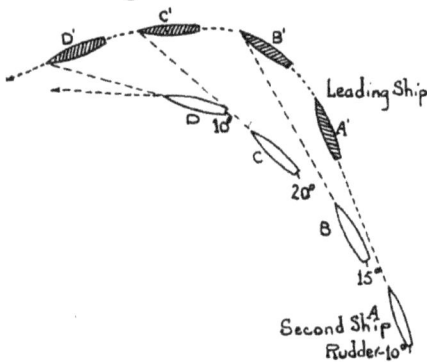

FIG. 29.—Gaining distance on a turn—3d method.

In Fig. 29 a third method is illustrated. It may be used when it is desired to gain from 100 to 50 yards. Start the turn simultaneously with the ship ahead and keep your jack staff pointed on her bow or other selected point throughout the turn. You will put the rudder over very slowly at first (A) and increase the angle gradually until at the middle of the turn yu have about standard rudder (B and C). You will then start to ease it (D) and bring it slowly to amidships. You gain some ground by turning inside and more by averaging less rudder than the leading ship.

It is very easy to gain ground on a countermarch. In Fig. 30 the leading ship begins to turn with standard rudder at X. The second ship is 250 yards behind proper station (A). You commence the turn with standard rudder at B, 125 yards before reaching the normal point for turning X. You will be in correct position at the end of the turn (C).

It is not good practice to try to lose distance by turning late and outside. Once you get only a few yards outside the wake, it will hold you out even if you increase the rudder angle to 28 degrees. In addition to ending up well beyond the new track of the column, almost always you will lose more distance than you desired and come out as far behind station as you were ahead.

In maneuvers it is well to have a good man assigned to the engine-room annunciators, bell pulls, faster and slower indicators, and at night the speed light. He also mans the voice tube to the gun-control station. This frees the captain from any manual work and lets him concentrate his attention on handling the ship.

Chasing torpedoes is a task frequently assigned to destroyers. There are many different methods of beginning the chase—due to the form of the torpedo practice—but once you get in the torpedo's wake the procedure is the same. Last winter three destroyers were assigned to chase torpedoes for a division of light cruisers. On each run one ship fired a salvo of three straight shots with the tube pointed approximately on her beam.

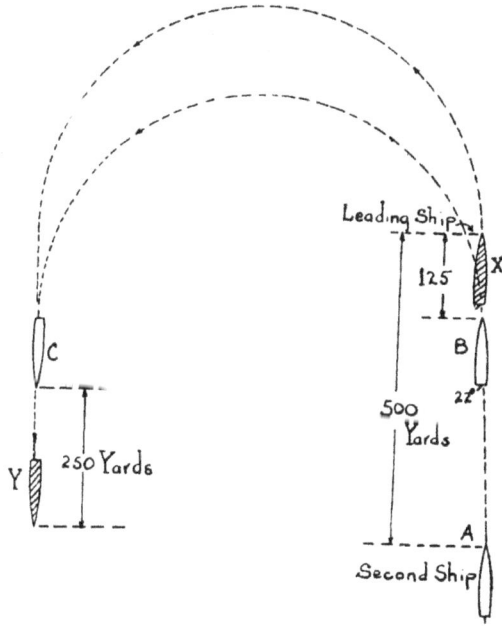

FIG. 30.—Gaining distance on a countermarch.

Shortly before the time to fire the three destroyers fell in astern of the cruiser in column at close distance—no exact distance was prescribed. When the torpedo salvo was fired all destroyers turned to follow it—the leading boat with nearly full rudder and the others with less. The leading ship crossed the tracks of all three torpedoes during her turn and thus was able to see that all were running properly. She chased the farthest torpedo, hoisting the appropriate flag signal. When these flags were flown from all destroyers it proved that the chase had been started correctly. After that each destroyer was responsible for the torpedo she was chasing. Up to this time destroyer speed should equal torpedo speed.

It is well to be about 250 yards behind the torpedo at the beginning of the chase. Then take off twenty turns and at the end of the chase you will be about 1,000 yards in rear—the track can be seen easily at this distance when exactly astern of the torpedo. If more than 250 yards astern when the chase begins decrease speed only fifteen or ten turns, the object always being to end up at 1,000 yards distance when the torpedo makes its first broach at the end of the run. At the first opportunity line the ship up with the torpedo track to get the compass course. Then, if compelled to stop or slow down, you will know the exact direction in which to resume the chase. Have officers in the top and on the gun-control platform to keep the torpedo track in sight. As soon as the torpedo first broaches slow down progressively and stop when distant 500 yards from the torpedo. This avoids the bad engineering effects of a sudden reduction of speed. It also avoids overrunning the torpedo while it is circling and diving erratically at the end of the run. After stopping set the course to pass the torpedo fifty yards abeam, on the side where the boat is to be lowered. When nearly up to the torpedo back just enough to kill the headway. When the headway is reduced to three knots and the boat is nearly abreast of the torpedo, give the signal for lowering.

On occasion there may be a large number of torpedoes in the water. A destroyer can easily recover three. The wherry is perfectly good for holding a torpedo until another boat is available. Once a punt was used very effectively for this purpose in a fairly choppy sea; this gave our sailors something to talk about and enhanced the reputation of the two nimble seamen who manned the craft.

There are two general types of erratic runs. First, the torpedo may make an erratic turn at the beginning of the run and then run straight. In this case, the difficulty lies in detecting the turn, which may be made during the deep initial dive, and in getting the ship turned into the torpedo's track. Once this is done, it is very important to get the course of the torpedo. The rest is easy. Second, the torpedo may run wild—turning, zigzagging, diving, and broaching—but keeping generally in the same area. Get clear about 1,000 yards and stop the engines. It is useless to try to follow a torpedo with a ship having many times its tactical diameter and you run the chance of chopping it in two with your propellers. If the torpedo heads toward you, just stay stopped. You have as good a chance of missing it that way as any other. We tried this out not so long ago. A torpedo was having a grand spree and we stopped to watch it from a distance which seemed safe. It curved around and straightened out for the bridge. It broached fifty yards short, dove beautifully under the ship and came up fifty yards on the other side. Let's hope all are as well trained.

Chapter XI

ENGINEERING OPERATION

One of the most important duties of the engineer officer is to determine the engineering set-up to be used at each speed. Steady steaming alone or a maximum variation of three turns from standard in formation is assumed. As an illustration of how this data may be tabulated, the following was compiled for a Squantum destroyer about three months after an excellent navy yard overhaul:

These data have, of course, many variations. They will differ much for individual ships, even of the same type. For the same ship they will vary in accordance with the general state of repair of the plant, the condition of the bottom, the temperature of sea water, the displacement of the ship, and the characteristics of the fuel oil. In addition to having such a table for favorable conditions—to give a mark to shoot at—the engineer should keep another copy corrected to date for actual daily use. As the Squantum boats are being scrapped, the above figures have, of course, no actual application. They are included to show the kind and extent of the data which the engineer officer should keep. Similar data for port steaming should be available.

When a standard speed is made effective the normal set-up for it is placed in operation. Turbine nozzles always are opened wide. If steaming singly, the throttle also is opened wide and the approximate revolutions obtained by varying the boiler steam pressure. It is unnecessary to make the exact revolutions constantly as long as the average is close to the standard speed. This system gives the navigator a little extra work for his dead reckoning but saves a lot of oil and effort below. When cruising in formation the throttle is closed very slightly, enough to give a drop of about ten pounds in steam pressure through it. This

Speeds	11.5	13	15	16	17	18	19	20.5	25	27	30
Boilers	2	2	2	2	13	15	2	2	3	3	4
Burners	7	9	12	11	13	15	18	21	34	44	48
Burner tips	1/16	1/16	1/16	3/32	3/32	3/32	3/32	3/32	3/32	3/32	7/64
Oil pressure	200	200	200	200	200	225	225	250	300	300	300
Boiler steam	225	250	180	200	215	225	240	250	250	250	250
Blowers	1	1	1	1	1	1	1	2	3	3-4	4-6
Blower nozzles	0	0	1	1	1	2	2	0	2-3	3	3
Feed pumps in use	1 aux	1 aux	1 aux	1 aux	1 main	1 main	1 main	1 main	1 main	1 main	2 main
Feed pump strokes	9	10	11	12	13	14	15	15	16	18	20
Turbine nozzles	0	0	#1	#1	#1	#2	#3	#3	#1-5	#1-7	#1-8
Air pump strokes	9	9	10	10	12	13	14	15	16	19	22
Exhaust trunk temp.	92	89	96	96	96	98	105	108	112	117	125

excess pressure in the boilers and main steam lines up to the throttles causes a slight reduction in economy, but is necessary to give a small reserve of steam if a few extra turns must be added temporarily. It allows a steady boiler steam pressure to be maintained.

When the ship is steadied down in position fuel-oil meters are read hourly and the engineering score determined. If this is not satisfactory slight changes are made in the set-up or an alternate one tried. The best set-up can usually be determined in three hours; this then is used for the duration of the run. After running in formation for a few hours the average revolutions to keep the ship in position are determined and used as the standard speed.

Certain speeds are manifestly uneconomical. In Squantum boats those just under eleven knots were bad because the circulating pumps had to be started. Similarly those just above twenty-one knots were very wasteful in oil because the engines had to be run in parallel. Speeds between thirteen and fifteen knots were unsatisfactory because one turbine nozzle had to be opened and to leave the throttle wide open it was necessary to reduce the steam pressure below 180 pounds—generally considered about the low limit. Many destroyers vibrate badly at certain speeds, notably between eighteen and twenty-one knots. Such uneconomical or vibrating speeds should be avoided whenever possible.

When making high speeds in formation or carrying out gunnery exercises, it is desirable to have a considerable reserve of steam to provide for unforeseen contingencies. This results in a loss of economy, but at such time that must be subordinated to more important considerations.

When leaving another ship or dock the boiler steam pressure should be raised close to the safety valve settings. One blower will be sufficient except in unusually difficult situations, where prolonged high-power maneuvering seems probable. In fact, during the last year of destroyer command, I cannot remember a case where we used two blowers.

When landing alongside a ship or dock, the reduction of steam during the approach will bring the steam pressure up and give ample reserve power. When unusually difficult conditions and prolonged high-power maneuvering are expected you may start an additional blower. But for nine out of ten landings one blower will be ample and you are wasting oil to start another—to say nothing of the terrific din they raise.

During periods of gunnery training requiring full power the division commander should inform his ships well in advance of the times when full power will be required, and also when it will no longer be required that day. If there is a prospective interval of any duration between two runs at high power one fireroom can be cut out and the boilers left with steam formed. This effects economy both in oil and personnel. The boilers can be cut in again on fifteen minutes' notice. Sometimes the need for full power will arise sooner than can be foreseen, but in a pinch you can always start out with two boilers and cut in the others during the acceleration. We have done this with a Squantum boat and of course it would be much easier with other types, where two boilers will give you almost twenty-seven knots.

When lying to with engines stopped one boiler should be cut out and, if well clear of other vessels or shoals, one main air pump, two lubricating oil pumps, and other machinery may be stopped. The steam pressure can be dropped to 150 pounds. Under such conditions you must keep a good watch for other vessels approaching.

If necessary, fifteen knots can be made on one boiler. It provides sufficient power for shifting from one anchorage to another or to leave from alongside a ship and anchor. A simple landing alongside another ship can be made with one boiler, but, if time and other conditions permit, it is well to wait until a second is ready. One boiler and one engine are ample for sighting anchors in the Yangtze and can be used for shifting berth in an emergency. As a choice between two evils I would rather attempt a maneuver with one boiler or one engine than warm them too rapidly.

During a month's cruise in the Kurile Islands it was necessary to stand by much of the time when at anchor because of the very erratic weather. The plan usually employed was first to raise the steam pressure on one boiler to 200 pounds and warm one engine. When the weather grew very threatening, the second engine was warmed and steam pressure raised to 250 pounds. In exceptionally dangerous situations, when high power would be required instantly should the anchor drag or the chain part, a second boiler was cut in and the boiler pressure reduced as much as we dared. This economy was essential for the execution of our mission—not to make a good engineering score. Incidently, as we grew accustomed to the conditions, the times and extent of standing by were much reduced. Closer acquaintance reduces the terror of any menace.

About the shortest time I remember for lighting off an extra boiler, boosting it and the auxiliary boiler to 250 pounds, and actually getting under way is sixteen minutes. This, of course, is not the best thing in the world for the engineering plant and is recommended only when the safety of the ship demands it.

For steady steaming it is more economical to steam on two boilers than one, even at the lowest speeds. Again, there is no advantage in steaming on one engine, as is done by submarines. However, if necessary because of casualty, the economy is not much reduced, provided the other propeller is allowed to turn freely. In case of a turbine casualty the injured engine should be locked so that it cannot turn and cause more damage. Steaming, of course, is very uneconomical under these conditions, and seven or eight knots is as much as you can make good. The ship naturally is very difficult to handle. Once after running all night and creeping through the channel into Norfolk, we gave the yard pilot and tug waiting for us off the city a hearty welcome.

While waiting for the commencement of a high-speed run in formation, it is well for the engineer or his assistant to stay on the bridge. There he can get first-hand information of the situation as it develops and make his preparations accordingly.

Incidently, neither the engineer nor his assistant should stand deck watches under way; both should give their entire attention to engineering. One of them should spend at least one hour of every night watch in their department when under way.

A constant watch on the smoke telegraphs is essential to engineering efficiency but, unless stood by well-trained men, this is useless. Appreciable steady light black smoke, without heat waves, should be coming from all stacks at all times. It is all very well to say you want a light brown haze, but such orders will result in a clear stack most of the time. Get some smoke you can actually see—that there is no question about. In a year's time we certainly cut in half the steam used in our blowers and increased boiler efficiency very considerably due to elimination of excess air.

The captain should make it his personal responsibility to see that the propellers are not bent or even nicked. When entering port and even at sea a constant watch should be kept for floating logs and obstructions. These are particularly noticeable in New York harbor. True most of them will be floating horizontally and will pass over the propeller blades, but sometimes a log will be weighted at one end, which may be several feet underwater. Even the small fish stakes floating about Manila Bay will put a good nick in the edge of the blade. In clear water take a look at your propellers frequently. In dark water have them examined from time to time by a diver. Have this man scrape off all barnacles and grass. The same should be done for the main injections. These frequently become clogged with seaweed, or more probably with old clothes or refuse thrown over the side. Oily water and coffee should not be thrown over the side, but poured down the drain from the head. An additional reason for this procedure was the losing of several oil heater fittings which were lying in a bucket of oil—they went over the side with the oil. In consequence we went without a heater for over a month, or rather shifted the parts from one heater to the other as we changed firerooms. We seem to have drifted into rather small details, but sometimes they have proved important and they may again.

Chapter XII

LANDING ALONGSIDE ANOTHER DESTROYER

This is probably the most interesting phase in the art of destroyer handling. Every situation is different and each has potential, if not actual, difficulties. And the potential have a way of becoming actual. When leaving another vessel or a dock you must make one continuous maneuver—the quicker it is completed the better. You start from a safe position and want to get clear before outside conditions can change it much. In making a landing, on the other hand, conditions are reversed— you want to get into that safe position. Therefore, take things easy—usually there is no reason for speed. Keep your ship well in hand and well clear—have the situation always under your control. Do things so slowly that you can see all that is happening and recognize the beginning of a bad situation, while there is still time to rectify your error. Try to keep the ship in such a position that a single error will not result in a poor landing, for you are liable to make that single error. Always keep your plans one step ahead—have a scheme ready to meet every contingency and to rectify every error. You can only do this if you keep events marching slowly, unless you happen to be one of those ship handlers who are born, not made. Of course, there are times in strong winds and currents when "strong-arm" methods are necessary. Then it is actually safest to come in fast; in fact, it often is the only way to do the job. Usually there will be enough landings of this kind to keep you in good practice. If not, try out a fast landing from time to time under easy conditions to keep your hand in. But, except for this purpose, do not make a fast landing unless necessary— for you cannot then follow all the action, you cannot keep your plans projected into the future, and you cannot rectify your errors. In a fast landing you must use the best plan and execute it almost perfectly—there is no room for errors. So, in making your landings, do not make any unnecessary risks for yourself. Enough of them will be forced upon you by the gods of the winds and tides. Don't come up to them with a chip on your shoulder and dare them to knock it off—for they will.

As you approach the landing make a careful estimate of the situation. Take into effect every factor—force and direction of wind and current; yaw or swing of the other destroyer; displacement and trim of your own ship; and the obstructions in your desired line of approach. Decide upon the manner of making the approach, the track to be followed, the speed to be used, the angle there should be between your final approach course and the keel of the other destroyer, and whether you will make a close, medium, or wide landing. A close landing means about five yards between ships; a medium, ten; and a wide landing, fifteen yards.

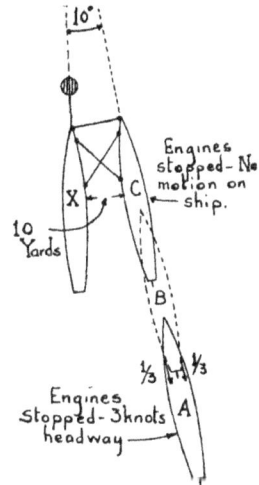

FIG. 31.—Normal landing.

It is vitally important to get a long straight approach. Get straightened out on your final course at least five hundred yards from the other ship. An approach which involves a last minute change of course doubles or triples the difficulties of the landing. I venture to say that half the poor landings are caused by failure to get a long straight approach. This is one time when you should beware of short cuts. Take five minutes more and start from the right position. In the long run you will even save time, to say nothing of oil and reputation.

Let's begin with a simple landing under normal conditions— no appreciable wind or current and no obstructions in the line of approach (Fig. 31). Approach at a 10-degree angle to the other destroyer X for a medium landing. Reduce speed so as to have three knots headway when your bow passes the other destroyer's stern (*A*). When your bridge is abreast the search-light platform (*B*), back both engines one-third. Stop them so that the ship will be dead in the water when abreast the other vessel. Remember that a heavy ship keeps her way much longer than a light one and make due allowance for a very heavy or light condition. Curtis turbines spin quite a few seconds after the throttle is closed. So order "stop" when you are still going ahead at about half a knot. If you wait until the ship is dead in the water, you will get sternway on the ship. With Parsons turbines the action is quicker, but it will probably take five seconds from the order until the propeller stops.

When your stem is abreast the forecastle gun, the heaving lines for the three forecastle lines are thrown and the lines run out quickly. Train your people to throw the lines toward the part of the other ship where the mooring lines are to be secured. Do not let the throws be made until this can be done and it is certain that the lines will reach. This will save time in the end and conduce to the safety and smartness of the landing. If it is desired to make doubly certain of getting out the bow line quickly, have two heaving lines ready for it. Have the heaving line made fast to the exact center of the mooring line's eye-splice, so that it will not catch on other mooring lines or in the chocks. Usually there is no particular hurry about the stern line. Get it out when within easy heaving line distance, taking care that it is kept clear of the propeller.

In most cases, when stopped in position *C*, the ship will come in of its own accord. Should the bow get in too close, it is easy to bring it out by twisting the ship with the engines (Fig. 32). If you are a bit too far astern (Case 1), send the inboard engine ahead two-thirds, back the outboard engine one-third, and put the rudder outboard (*A*). As the ship moves ahead at about one knot it will soon come parallel (*B*). In emergency use more power—port ahead standard, starboard astern two-thirds; or even, port ahead full, starboard astern full.

Should the ship be a little ahead of position and it be necessary to bring the bow out (Case 2), go ahead one-third with the inboard engine, back the outboard engine one-third, and put the rudder inboard (C). This will send the ship astern at about 1-knot speed and into a parallel position (D). In emergency use more power.

If the other ship is secured to a mooring buoy of the large flat type, such as used at Charleston, you can often hold your bow out temporarily by letting it ride against this buoy (Case 3, position E). This works very effectively when the other destroyer is riding ahead of the buoy, so that it will come between the two ships (Case 4, position F). It is well not to rely too

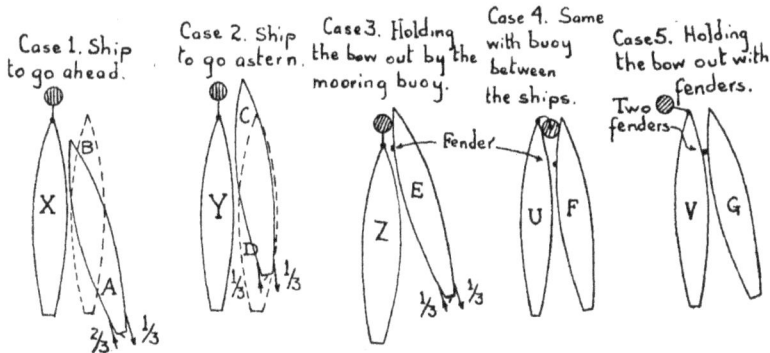

FIG. 32.—Getting the bow out.

much on this expedient when winds or currents are very strong or when you are at an angle of over 20 degrees with the other ship. It should not be attempted when the buoy is of the can type—as used principally at Newport. In any case, it is only a temporary measure. As soon as possible twist the ship into a parallel position by the methods shown in Cases 1 and 2.

Should you see that your forecastle is bound to come in contact with the other ship—which never should occur with skillful handling—put over your cylindrical rope fender opposite No. 1 gun and get all fore-and-aft motion off the ship (Case 5, position G). Then the other ship can put one of its small fenders against your cylindrical fender. These two fenders together will hold the ships well apart and no stanchions will be bent.

Now assume that the stern gets in too close during the landing. Because of possible injury to the propellers it should be brought out immediately. A number of methods are shown in Fig. 33. If the bow line is out, heave in on it with the capstan (Case 1). As the bow comes in the stern moves out. If bow line is not out, pass over No. 2 line quickly. Go ahead one-third with the outboard engine, put the rudder inboard, and hold the line (Case 2). If no forward lines are immediately available, send the outboard engine ahead two-thirds with full inboard rudder; if the inboard propeller is well clear, back that engine one-third (Case 3). In all these maneuvers the stern line, if out, should be kept entirely slack.

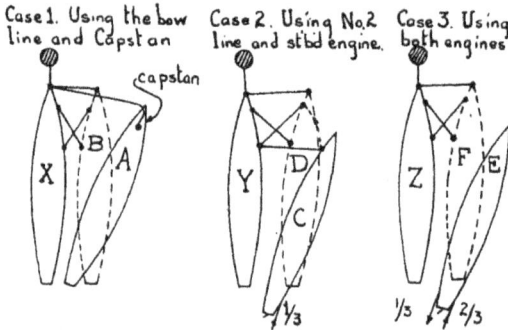

FIG. 33.—Getting the stern out.

Perhaps, after your ship has come to a stop abreast the other destroyer, she will show no tendency to come in. It will be necessary to spring her in with lines and engines (Fig. 34). Case 1 shows the method of most general application. Take the bow line to the capstan. Back the outboard engine one-third and alternate the inboard engine be-

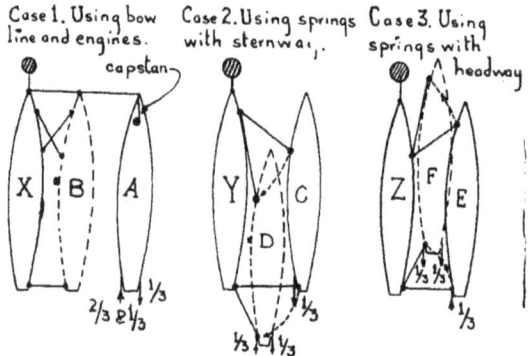

FIG. 34.—Bringing the ship in.

tween one- and two-thirds ahead to keep fore-and-aft motion off the ship (A). Heave in the bow line as necessary to keep the ship parallel. She will come in bodily. When there is about ten feet between your big fender and the side of the other destroyer, stop the engines (*B*) and the momentum will bring her alongside.

You can also bring the ship in by holding forward and after lines simultaneously and kicking the ship ahead or astern with an engine (Cases 2 and 3). The disadvantage of these methods lies in the fact that you have not direct control over the stern line and must rely on a rather uncertain line of communications. And remember that both forward and after lines must be held. The desired result will most certainly not be produced by holding a forward line alone.

In Case 2 hold No. 3 and the stern line, and kick the inboard engine one-third astern (*C*). To keep the ship parallel as she comes in you must ease out No. 3 line gradually. A glance at the figure will show that there is more of this line out in position *D* than in *C*. When the ship is sprung into position *D*, kick the engines ahead one-third to bring her into correct position for securing.

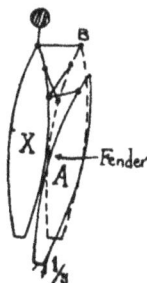

In Case 3 hold No. 2 and the stern line, and and kick the inboard engine ahead one-third (*E*). Ease out gradually on No. 2 line to keep the ship parallel. When the ship is sprung into position *F* kick both engines astern one-third to bring her into correct position.

FIG. 35.—Correcting too close a landing.

When alongside with all lines out, but the ship is not in exactly the right fore-and-aft position, kick one engine ahead or astern while you count five. Hold the lines a little before the ship reaches the right position. After you have secured, most of the strain will come on No. 3 line. Therefore, before doubling up, have the ship one or two feet ahead of position. This will allow for a little stretch in the line. See that No. 2 line is taut, so that swells of passing ships will not permit the vessel to surge forward. When doubling up see that the strain is equally divided among all the three parts of each line. If you expect to remain alongside for several days, put canvas around the lines where they pass through the chocks to prevent chafing.

Next take the case of too close a landing (Fig. 35). While ship still has about two knots way on, the big fender makes contact with the other ship's side opposite her searchlight platform. As a result of this contact your bow will go out rather sharply and the stern will come in. As the ship forges ahead, the fender continuing to rub, there is danger of your inboard propeller hitting. Therefore, stop the inboard engine immediately. Pass your No. 2 line across quickly without a heaving line and hold it. Go ahead one-third with the outboard engine with full inboard rudder (*A*). This will bring you back into a parallel position and swing the stern clear (*B*). By all means do not touch the inboard engine. If the propellers touch when stopped, little, if any, damage will result.

Let us now introduce the factors of current and wind into our problem. If there is a current from ahead (Fig. 36), make a wide landing at a 5-degree angle. Bring the ship dead in the water opposite the other destroyer. The current, slightly on the outboard bow, will bring you in gently against the other destroyer, allowing plenty of time to get all the lines out and well in hand. Kick ahead with an engine sufficiently to keep abreast while waiting for the current to bring you in. When almost alongside a kick ahead with the inboard engine or a brief twist with both will bring you parallel. Watch the No. 3 line carefully and hold it when the ship is a yard or two ahead of position. The ship will ride to this line and in doubling up you will lose a foot or two; the stretch of the lines will drop you back in exact position. It is a lot easier to drop the ship back by slacking this line than to get steam on the capstan and haul the ship ahead against the current. This type of landing is an easy one unless the current is very strong. The *Pope* made such a landing at Hankow against a 5-knot current, but the conditions were difficult. Had the current been stronger the landing would have involved great risk of injury to both ships.

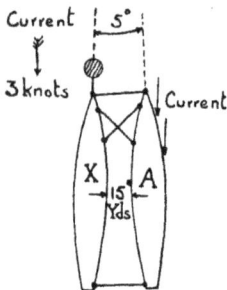

FIG. 36.—Landing against a current.

A strong wind from ahead will have little effect on a good landing, but will exaggerate the effect of errors in handling the ship. Make a medium landing at an angle of 5 degrees or less. Keep pointed closely into the wind during the approach and landing. Should the bow show a tendency to come in, counteract this quickly by twisting the ship with the engines.

A strong wind at right angles to a moderate current does not add much to the difficulty of the problem, but makes it necessary to take certain precautions. Suppose the wind from the west and current from the north (Fig. 37). The other destroyer X will head about 340 degrees, with the current about 20 degrees on her starboard bow. When making a landing against her starboard side the current will set you in strongly. Its effect will be much greater than the holding-off effect of the wind, the force of which will be broken by the other ship when in her lee. Try for a parallel and extra wide landing at extreme heaving line distance—twenty to twenty-five yards. While gaining position for the approach, get a true bearing of the other ship when her masts are in line—or at least estimate her true heading. Steer this course during the approach—with

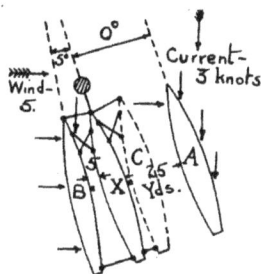

FIG. 37.—Landing in cross wind and current.

your ship pointed well to the right of the other vessel. Have the navigator take a series of true bearings of the starboard wing of her bridge. Determine from them whether you are being set in too much or too little toward her. Always make a greater allowance for the current than these bearings indicate, because it will have a relatively greater effect when you stop the engines to coast alongside. Too great an allowance will merely delay your landing a few minutes. Too small an allowance will result in a dangerous situation or a failure to make the landing. If your bearings indicate that you are going to end up too far outside, decrease speed during the approach to allow the current to set you in more and stop the engines earlier than usual. If you find that the current is setting you in more than expected, increase the speed during the approach to decrease the effect of the current and stop the engines later than usual. In the last case it will probably be necessary to back two-thirds or even full. Such high backing powers introduce an element of danger, because it is probable that one engine will start to back quicker than the other or accelerate faster, thus twisting the ship from its parallel position.

Assuming that you come alongside at the correct distance (A), the current will gradually sweep you down alongside about the time your lines are out and ready for holding (C). During this time it may be necessary to go ahead one-third with either engine to keep abreast or to twist the ship with both engines to keep parallel. As an indication of what can be accomplished under unfavorable conditions of wind and tide a landing of the *Pope* in Kashiwabara Wan, Kurile Islands, will be cited. The current was three knots. The wind was howling down from the snow-covered volcanoes at force-seven. There was an angle of about 45 degrees between wind and tide. The handling was perfect. A medium parallel landing was made. The ships came together with quite a heavy shock—it was well they were exactly parallel. In addition to the difficulty of the actual situation the captain was confronted by a serious mental hazard—there was no navy yard nearer than about 3,000 miles and casualty might have caused the failure of the Army World Flight. I have seen few landings as fine as this one.

Now assume that you are required to come alongside with your starboard side toward the other destroyer. Use a 5-degree approach to a close landing with more than normal headway (B). Back one-third, increasing to two-thirds if necessary. When you get alongside the current will tend to push your bow out, an effect which will be partly counteracted by the wind. Be prepared to twist the ship with high power. Speed in getting out the lines is very essential. It is not difficult to get the ship into the proper position. The real problem is to hold her there until the lines are out and ready for use.

Often ships or obstructions will be in your normal line of approach. This will compel an unfavorable angle of approach and a sharp turn with outboard rudder just before coming alongside (Figs. 38 and 39). Approach at the smallest angle which will clear the obstructions *YZ* and try for a wide landing. Instead of backing both engines, go astern one- or two-thirds with the outboard engine and outboard rudder (*A*, Figs. 38 and 39). This will swing the ship. If the angle of approach was not too great nor the current or wind from ahead too strong it will bring you parallel (*B*, Fig. 38). If it

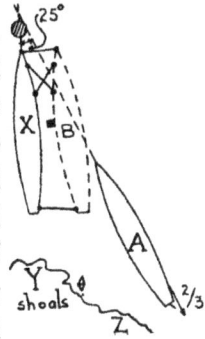

Fig. 38.—Landing with obstruction in line of approach.

does not do so, continue backing the outboard engine two-thirds and go ahead two-thirds or standard on the inboard engine, placing the rudder amidships (*B*, Fig. 39). As a final resort twist the ship with full power. There are very few conditions under which this will not pull your bow out and bring the ship parallel (*C*, Fig. 39). By these methods a 50- to 60-degree landing without wind or current is quite easy. A 30- to 40-degree landing with current or strong breeze from ahead requires skill and the use of power, but is not very difficult. A 90-degree landing without wind or current was once made without difficulty, but it took some minutes and consumed considerable fuel (Fig. 40). During such

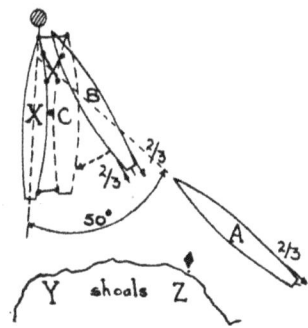

Fig. 39.—Landing with obstruction in line of approach at a greater angle of approach.

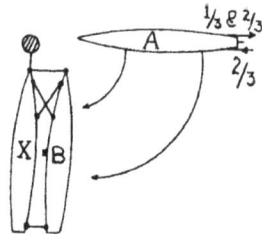

Fig. 40.—Landing with a 90-degree angle of approach.

landings it is absolutely necessary to avoid taking any strain whatever on the forecastle lines until the ships are parallel.

A particularly difficult type of landing is one which requires a large turn—maybe as much as 90 degrees—very close under the stern of another destroyer X to go along its farther side (Fig. 41). It is a remarkable feat to make a direct landing under these conditions; i.e., to go directly from B to F. Often there will not be room enough for such a turn between the other ship X and the obstructions YZ astern of it. Usually the most

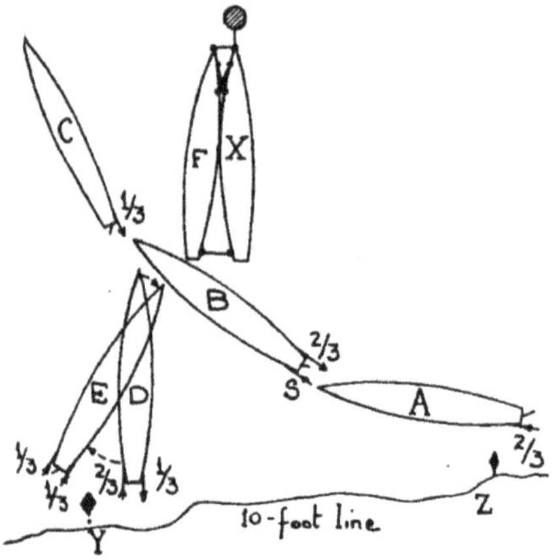

Fig. 41.—90-degree turn under the stern of the other ship before landing.

practicable method is to make a sharp turn with rudder and engines close under the stern (A) and (B) and come up abreast and nearly parallel to the other ship about fifty to one hundred yards away (C). Then back down slowly with the inboard engine and outboard rudder as far as the shoals permit (D). Now kill your sternway and twist the ship with both engines until it points about at the bridge of the other ship (E). Then go ahead one-third speed on a curving track with outboard rudder to a normal landing (F).

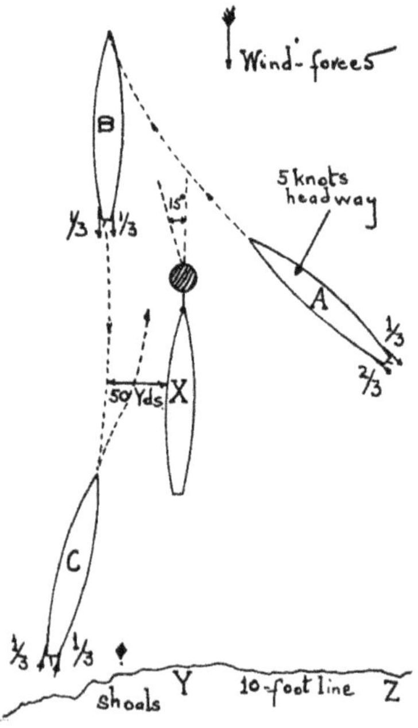

Fig. 42.—A backing landing—an alternate method of solving the problem of Fig. 41.

Often the problem presented in Fig. 41 can be solved more easily by a backing landing (Fig. 42). This is not difficult unless there is a strong wind or a current. Approach with good headway from as favorable a direction as possible (A). From this position commence a sharp turn with engines and rudder at about five knots across the bow of the other destroyer and well clear. Bring the ship to a stop in a position about 15 degrees on her farther bow (B). If not yet parallel, continue twisting the ship with the engines to bring her so. Then back down with both engines and slight outboard rudder. Pass the other ship on a slightly curving track at about fifty yards. When you have gone astern as far as the obstructions permit (C), go ahead one-third both engines and make the landing in the usual way. Use a leadsman aft. In case of a strong current from ahead, give the other ship an extra wide berth when passing her bow. When the wind is blowing strongly from ahead use seven or eight knots while passing from A to B and keep headway on the ship at B until you are pointed into the wind. In backing be careful to keep the ship pointed closely into the wind. If you give the breeze a chance it will get your bow in its grip and blow it off to one side. If the ship gets out of control in this way the only escape is to anchor.

In all landings be specially careful of your inboard propeller. If there is possibility of its contact with anything be sure to stop the engine in ample time. Always have steam on the capstan and your bow line around it, ready to heave in quickly should your stern get in too close.

Two destroyers can lay alongside in quite a heavy sea or a long ground swell provided they point into it. In the open roadstead of Hitokappu Wan, Kurile Islands, the *Ford* fueled from the *Pope* for several hours while a force-five breeze was blowing from seaward. As the wind kept increasing and the sea lengthened out the ships began to pound heavily and it was necessary to shove off. Later the *Pope* came alongside the *Ford* in the open roadstead of Kujira Wan. A severe gale had just ended and a long ground swell was running in from seaward. At first the swell was on the beam; the ships rolled heavily and parted a wire line. However, after swinging into the swell, they rode rather easily and remained together for several hours. Even then it was not considered safe to pass between the ships, but large quantities of provisions were pitched across. Under such conditions keep the lines rather slack and well protected by chafing gear. Wire lines have not sufficient elasticity and should not be used.

Chapter XIII

LANDING ALONGSIDE LARGE SHIPS

Landings alongside large ships usually are easier than alongside destroyers. Their sides are high and clear and their propellers usually are much less exposed. Also, due to greater draft a large ship will head more nearly into the current when a strong cross wind is blowing. It is not necessary to repeat the descriptions of the types of landings already covered, for they are very similar regardless of the kind of ship you are going alongside. Several special types of landings will be described.

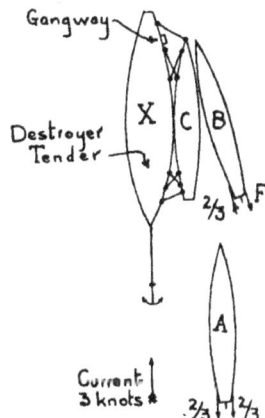

Frequently it will be necessary to make a bow-to-stern landing alongside a tender to shift a propeller or hoist out a turbine. Such a landing is easy if the tender is riding into a wind, even a strong one. But if it is riding to a strong current, then you have a difficult task to accomplish (Fig. 43). You must approach with the current, and there is a strong probability that it will catch your stern and sweep it out while you are trying to get alongside. Try for a medium parallel landing. Make special

Fig. 43.—A bow-to-stern landing alongside a tender with a strong current.

preparations for getting a stern line over quickly. Have several heaving lines ready so one certainly will get across. One should be thrown from the after deck house because of its higher position. Be ready to bend two mooring lines together. Make the approach with just steerage way on the ship. Because of the current, back two-thirds or even full (A) in time to stop the ship in the proper position. If possible, stop backing the inboard engine before its propeller is abreast the bow of the other ship, to avoid having your stern wedged out by the screw current. If your stern starts going out, as is very probable, hold the stern line until you are again parallel. Then also hold No. 2 line until you are alongside. If the stern line is not yet secured on the other ship, back full the outboard engine and go ahead two-thirds the inboard engine (B). This will bring the ship parallel and give her about three knots sternway to hold her in position against the current (C). If you should be too far out now for a heaving line to reach, get the stern in a little and kick the engines astern enough to keep abreast, allowing the current to bring you in slowly, as in Fig. 36.

If there is no current and the tender is riding into a moderate breeze any tendency of the stern to go out or in can be counteracted by backing the appropriate engine. The twisting effect thus created will be supplemented by the tendency to back into the wind.

Frequently a tender will leave its after gangway out— your stem will come just opposite it. There will be ample room if you keep the ship parallel, but you must not let the bow get canted in. The high overhang of the tender's forecastle will rip your upper works to pieces if you are swept in under it. For this reason it is safest to plan for a medium rather than a close landing, even though the latter will expedite the getting out of lines.

A landing with one engine is always difficult. The ship will steer fairly well at speeds above five knots, but once steerage way is lost, control is lost also, and cannot quickly be regained. This difficulty is emphasized when, due to a turbine casualty, it is necessary to clamp one shaft so the propeller does not move. When going ahead the clamped propeller will have the partial effect of backing. When, with these handicaps, you are required to make a bow to stern landing in a shifting current, you have one of the most difficult tasks which confronts a destroyer captain during peace time. Let us assume that the outboard engine alone is available (Fig. 44). To keep well clear of the tender's over-hanging bow make an extra wide landing. As you can back only the outboard engine, approach at a 10-degree angle, so that after you have brought the ship to a stop it will be about parallel. During the approach determine the effect of the current by steering a compass course and watching the change of compass bearing of a point on the large ship X. If it is setting you in make ample allowance for it. C and D illustrate what will occur if insufficient allowance is made for the current. Once the ship gets as far along as C, it is in a trap from which there is no escape. To stop, back, or go ahead leaves a choice only between different kinds and degrees of disaster, for you cannot avoid being swept under the tender's overhanging forecastle. It is perfectly designed to catch your bridge, foremast backstays, and amidship gun. Also, the propeller may foul her anchor chain. A wise precaution before making such a landing is to unhook and clear away the backstays

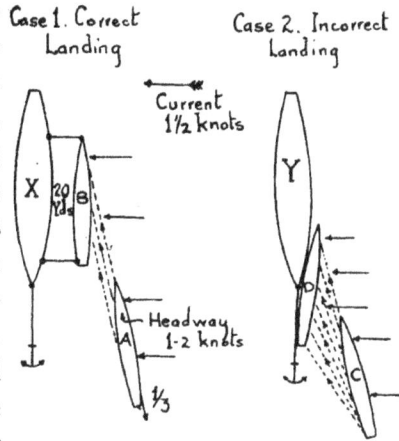

FIG. 44.—Bow-to-stern landing in a variable and shifting current.

which lead from the foretop and fore truck to the forward outboard corner of the amidship deck house. If they are caught in the step for the tender's lower boom, the topmast will come down, and perhaps even the lowermast.

But banish such unpleasant thoughts and let's see the best chances of avoiding such disasters. As said before, the wisest precaution is to make ample allowance for the current. When you think you have done so, double it. For when you slow down the effect of the current will be much greater. If your first bearings do not show current effect, keep taking them, particularly if the tide is just changing. Stop the engine when about 250 yards from your berth, so as to have one to two knots headway when your bow overlaps the other ship(A). Then back the outboard engine one-third with outboard rudder. This should bring you parallel (B). Get lines out quickly and work the ship in cautiously. In case anything goes wrong you can always go ahead with the outboard engine and get clear for another attempt.

Rather an unusual landing is illustrated in Fig. 45. An oiler X was fast aground on the eastern bank of Cooper River off Charleston. A 3- to 4-knot current was ebbing against her port bow. A moderate breeze was blowing from her port beam. A 15-foot shoal was in the direct line of approach. To avoid it two right-angled turns would be necessary. Two destroyers, *Sharkey* and *Putnam*, already had gone along her port side (Y and Z) after prolonged, high-power maneuvering of great difficulty and danger. A large mooring buoy was seventy-five yards 25 degrees on the *Putnam's* port quarter. A large red nun buoy was twenty-five yards 15 degrees on her port bow. It was a very dark night. The force, but not the direction, of the current was known.

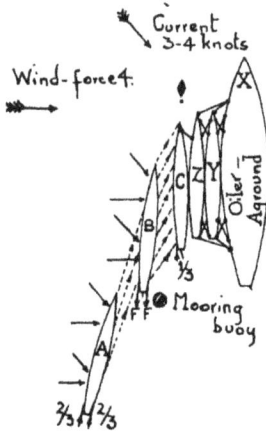

Fig. 45.—A difficult landing at night in Charleston.

The two buoys were illuminated by searchlights. We were warned to expect a strong set toward the other ships during the landing.

As a choice between two evils it was decided to make a straight approach directly across the 15-foot spot. Very liberal allowance was made for current and wind. To reduce their effect two-thirds speed was used and the course set so as to pass about twenty-five yards outside the mooring buoy (A). As we were being set very strongly toward this buoy, speed could not be decreased until our stern cleared it—this probably was a blessing in disguise, but the disguise was a good one. Then both engines were put from two-thirds ahead to full astern (*B*). The ship came to a stop parallel to and about five yards off the *Putnam*, but with our stem opposite her forecastle gun, fifteen yards too far astern. We had backed a few seconds too long. Under such conditions it requires extremely fine judgment to stop the engines at exactly the correct second. There seems to be an impelling tendency to give the order too late and thus stop the ship too soon, or even to get a little sternway on her. The current, in this case, carried us against the *Putnam* with considerable of a bang (*C*). The contact was taken entirely on our cane fender, but the bow came out somewhat. One-third ahead on the outboard engine, full inboard rudder, and a strain on No. 2 line swung the stern out quickly and brought the ship into proper position. Incidentally the three destroyers pulled the oiler off the shoal about midnight and brought her into a safe anchorage.

CHAPTER XIV

LANDING ALONGSIDE A DOCK

When there is neither wind nor current, landing alongside a dock is easier than alongside another ship. The forecastle and upper works are well above the level of the dock and usually there is nothing they can foul. If the bow touches first no damage will result unless there is considerable way on the ship or it makes quite an angle with the dock. The only way you can get into trouble is to let the stern touch first. Make a medium landing at a 10-degree angle with just steerage way on the ship. Do not throw heaving lines until you are almost opposite your assigned berth. Get them secured to the proper bollards from the start. Work the ship in gently. If you intend to take steam, electricity, and water, have the engineer officer tell you exactly where he wants the ship to make the connections. Get out all six lines with enough slack to allow for the rise and fall of the tide. In securing the gangway, see that a similar allowance is made, for it is easy to pull out a stanchion.

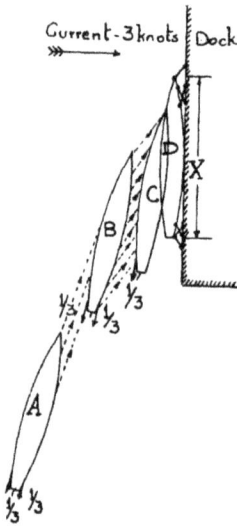

FIG. 46.—Landing along-side a dock with strong current setting on.

If there is a current as strong as one knot along the face of the dock, it is well to make the landing against it. Turn if necessary before coming alongside. Then the landing will be very simple.

A current or strong wind setting you toward the dock adds an element of interest to the problem, and sometimes one of difficulty. In Fig. 46 you are directed to secure in berth X. There are no other ships or obstructions to be considered.

A 3-knot current is setting you against the dock. Plan for an extra wide landing at a 10-degree angle. Make ample allowance for the effect of the current. Approach the dock at one-third speed (A). Hold this speed rather longer than usual because of the effect of the current, which will be increased when you decrease speed. When nearly opposite your berth back both engines one-third (B). When your bow is about five yards from the dock (C), stop the inboard engine. Continue backing the outboard engine and use outboard rudder to bring the ship parallel (D). During the approach watch the effect of the current and allow for it as necessary by altering the speed.

Fig. 47 shows a landing of this type which was made under somewhat difficult conditions. It was required to go alongside ship X at the coal dock at the Boston navy yard. Ahead of X was a very large floating crane (not shown in the figure) which extended nearly across the slip. We had followed ship X into port and had to wait some time until she had secured. As usual, this took just about twice as long as we had expected. In consequence we were swept far to the right by the 2-knot ebbing current. We had planned to make full allowance for that current by passing close to dock Y as we entered the slip. But, when we actually went in, we were

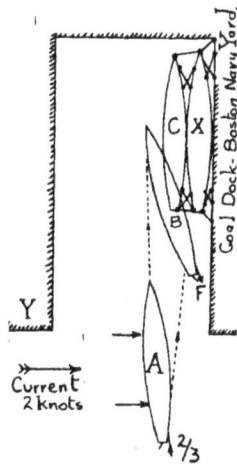

FIG. 47.—Landing— Boston navy yard in strong cross current.

closer to the other side (A) and in a very unfavorable position. However, having commenced the approach, it was decided to complete it. Considerations of prestige often compel one to attempt something which is hardly worth the risk involved. It evidently was necessary to do something radical. First, we must gain more room to the left against the current and get rid of its effect quickly. The rudder was put full left and the starboard engine sent ahead two-thirds (A). While this accomplished the purpose intended, it—together with the sweep of the current past the ends of the docks—carried our stern well toward the dock on our right. It also canted the ship very much from a parallel position. And it put about seven knots way on—we were pretty close to the crane ahead to be going at that speed. The consequences of ramming it imposed a mental hazard not to be underestimated. As the water was practically slack inside the slip—we had counted on this—the engine was stopped as soon as the stern was inside. In position B rudder was shifted full right and the starboard engine backed full speed. This had exactly the desired effect. The ship was twisted parallel and came to a little astern of position. She was then worked slowly into position C with engines and lines.

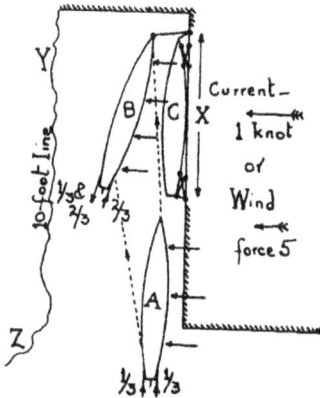

FIG. 48.—Landing with a strong current setting off from the dock.

This incident reënforced a lesson which had been taught often in the past. When a number of destroyers are securing to a dock before you, allow at least fifteen minutes for each ship to tie up. Keep half a mile off the dock until you can see that all is ready for your landing. When we entered Mobile with two divisions, the first three boats took about one and a half hours to secure. Suspecting that something like this would happen, we kept a mile downstream. Thus we could keep the ship pointed right by kicking an engine ahead occasionally and maintain our position against a gently ebbing current until signaled that the berth was ready.

Now let us tackle a really difficult problem—a landing where the ship is carried off the dock by a strong wind or moderate current. A typical situation is shown in Fig. 48. Make a 5-degree close landing with considerable way on the ship (A). Back two-thirds or full when your bow is opposite the middle of your assigned berth X. It is essential to get your bow line to the dock quickly. Have two heaving lines ready for use. If you can get the bow line out you can almost always make the landing. Make a special effort also with the stern line. If you can get it also to the dock, it will be much easier to bring the ship in against the current. If you have both lines out, hold them and go ahead or astern one-third both engines, thus bringing the ship in slowly, as in Cases 2 and 3, Fig. 34. If the stern line cannot be gotten out—which is to be expected— take the bow line to the capstan (B) and apply the method of Case 1, Fig. 34, with increased power. Put the inboard engine ahead two-thirds and alternate between one- and two-thirds astern with the outboard engine, keeping the ship in the same fore-and-aft position. As the bow is held by its line the ship will swing about it as a pivot and the stern will come in against the wind or current. After the ship is parallel to the face of the dock continue to handle the engines as before and heave in slowly with the bow line to keep the ship parallel as she comes in. In this way the ship can be brought in and placed in the exact position desired. If the current is strong it will be neces- sary to use standard speed ahead on the inboard engine and alternate between two-thirds and full astern on the outboard engine. If a pilot is available, ask him to put a tug on your port quarter to push the stern in.

If your heaving lines fall short, there is nothing to do but back out and try again. Don't hesitate too long to make this decision, or you may find yourself on the shoals YZ to the left.

Now let's forget the winds and currents for a while and put some obstructions along the dock. Often you will have to secure with your stem almost touching another vessel or a lighter. In this case bring the ship to a stop with twenty- five yards of open water ahead. Get out the lines and cautiously work ahead into proper position. Watch for some wild burst of speed by an overzealous engineer. You cannot emphasize too often the fact that when you ring one-third speed in close maneuvering, you want just that, and not a turn more.

Often it will be necessary to secure at a dock with other craft both ahead and astern—or about 110 yards of open space in which to put your 103 yards of ship, as berth X, Fig. 49. Make a wide landing well clear of the other ships Y and Z. Stop the ship about twenty-five yards off the dock and just opposite the berth (B). Get out the lines. If necessary throw them to other ships ahead and astern and have them passed to the dock. Work into position cautiously with engines and lines, bringing the bow in first (C). Make the final adjustments with the capstan.

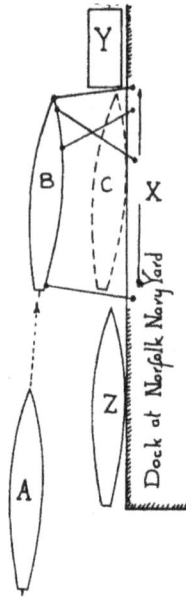

This last type of landing is very dangerous if we add a strong beam wind or current. The following is an actual situation. Six destroyers

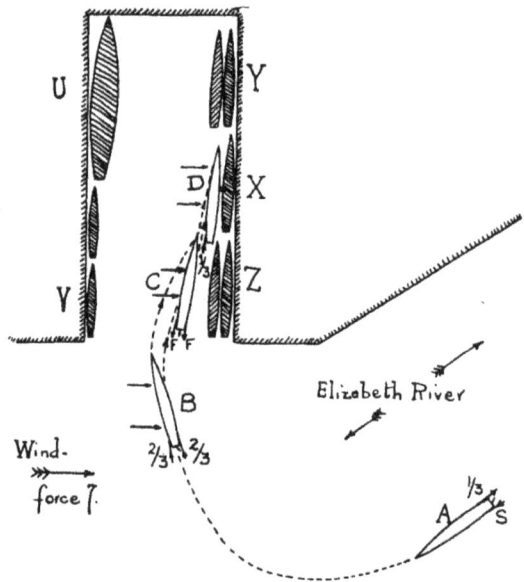

Fig. 49.—Landing between other craft.

were to be moored in pairs to a long dock in the Norfolk navy yard at a 135-degree angle to the Elizabeth River with starboard sides toward the dock (Fig. 50). A pair Y were moored

Fig. 50.—A difficult landing at the Norfolk navy yard in a strong beam wind.

at the inboard end of the dock. Astern of them was a single destroyer X. Astern of this boat was another pair of destroyers Z. Across the slip were a battleship and some small craft U and

V. There was very little maneuvering space in the slip—much less than shown in the sketch. A force-seven wind was blowing from the port beam. It was required to place the sixth destroyer alongside ship X.

The ship was very light, having only about 24,000 gallons of oil on board. During the approach a 135-degree turn to the right was made with the engines (A to B). As the ship straightened out (B) the force-seven wind became fully effective and blew her very strongly toward the outer pair of destroyers Z. To clear them it was necessary to go ahead two-thirds both engines. Even then there was not over ten yards to spare (C). In this position, as our bow overlapped the stern of the single destroyer X, both engines were backed full speed. Backing was continued a second or two too long, and the ship came to a stop ten yards too far astern.

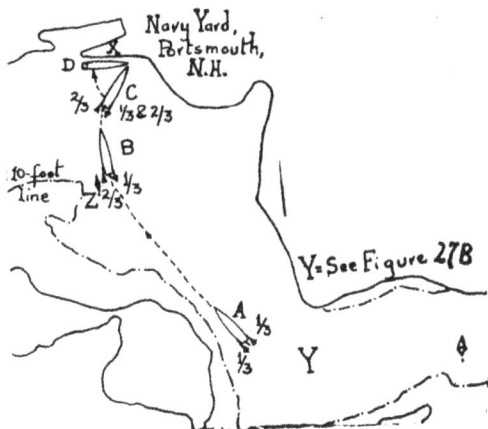

FIG. 51.—A turn and landing at the Portsmouth navy yard—no wind or current.

This caused the inboard propeller guard to touch slightly the outboard bow of the outer ship of the pair Z, but only after engines had been stopped and all way was off the ship (D). The outboard engine was kicked ahead one-third and the propeller guard quickly slid clear. The gale of wind blew the ship heavily against ship X in correct position. After securing, our bow was between sterns of the pair of destroyers ahead, overlapping them by about three feet. Our stern was about six feet from the stem of the destroyer astern. This is rather close quarters for full speeds in a gale of wind.

Occasionally it will be necessary to make a turn in narrow waters before coming alongside. In a current the only way to get around is to anchor (Fig. 23). If you have been able to select a time when the water is slack, you can usually get around by turning and twisting the ship with the engines. Fig. 51 shows such a turn and landing at the Portsmouth navy yard. The ship passed very close to the bank on the port hand at one-third speed (*A*). After the stern had cleared the buoy marking an outlying shoal *Z*, the speed of the port engine was increased to two-thirds and the starboard engine was backed one-third; the rudder was put full right (*B*). The ship then turned at easy headway into position *C*, where it made an angle of about 60 degrees with the dock. When the bow was about ten yards

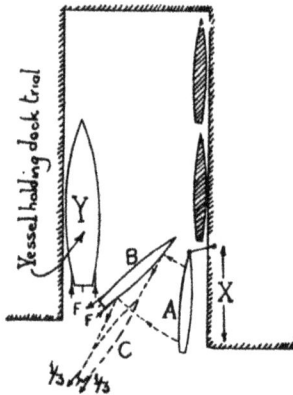

Fig. 52.—Effect of dock trial by another vessel.

off the bow line was gotten out and secured. The ship was sprung in with an engine twist (*C*), using the method of Fig. 48. As there was no current it was a simple problem to bring the ship alongside (*D*). Patience and care are the watchwords in such cases. Do everything deliberately and with low powers. Always have your plans projected one step in advance.

When making the approach to a navy yard dock note whether any vessels in the vicinity are conducting dock trials. Fig. 52 illustrates an incident which just escaped having serious consequences. A destroyer was ordered to secure to berth *X*. A large auxiliary *Y* was secured at the other side of the basin. It was conducting a dock trial. Her engines, going ahead at a high rate of speed, created a strong suction inside the basin. The destroyer came into position *A* and had a bow line out to the dock. The stern then showed a strong tendency to come out from the dock. The ship was twisted to quite an angle with the dock before it was realized that the suction current caused by the propellers of the other ship was responsible for this motion. The bow lin⸱ was cast off and the ship was twisted with full engine power i the attempt to swing the stern clear (B). About all that could be done was to maintain the same position, with about fifteen yards between the ships. We remained in this very dangerous position for some minutes, until our executive officer called over to the other ship and they stopped their engines. Then we backed off (C) and made another approach to the landing.

Often a destroyer entering a navy yard will be required to make a landing which is virtually impracticable without outside assistance. Do not disdain to receive the assistance of a pilot and his tugs in such cases, and to turn over the complete control of the ship to him. I have seen the pilots at Boston and Norfolk make some unbelievably skillful landings. On the other hand, the use of tugs without a pilot is not recommended. Ask them very politely to stand by in case you should get into some unforeseen trouble.

When there is a sharp curve in a river the current will carry you toward the bank on the outer arc of the curve. If you are required to land at a dock parallel to that bank against a strong current expect to find it decidedly on your outboard bow. A strong wind against your outboard side will reënforce this pushing-in effect of the current. Such a situation was met in going along the

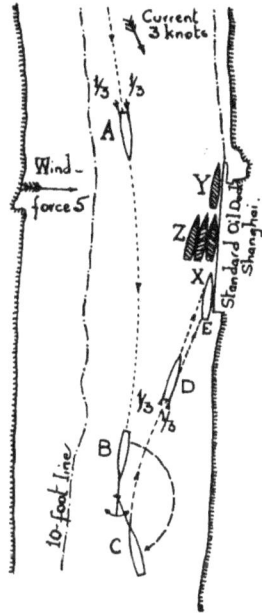

FIG. 53.—Landing in strong wind and current at Shanghai.

Standard Oil Dock at Shanghai (Fig. 53). Over the top of this sketch the river curves sharply to the left. In consequence the current, as indicated by the arrow, pushed the ship to the right in the same way as in Fig. 27B. Every one of the six destroyers which made the landing failed to make sufficient allowance for the effect of wind and current. Each came up against the dock or destroyer she was securing alongside before reaching her proper position—and practically every captain could be called an expert in handling destroyers.

Our ship, the *John D. Ford*, was fifth in column. She stood up at one-third speed past the dock (*A*), anchored in position *B*, and swung round the anchor into the current (*C*). She was under way and headed toward the dock (*D*) well before the fourth ship, which had turned with her engines, was up. We could therefore take the berth next to the dock *X*, which was much easier to land alongside than a destroyer. The first three destroyers had already secured abreast at *Z* and they constituted a mental hazard which tended to a slower approach than if the space ahead had been clear. This error, combined with a failure to allow enough for the effect of wind and current, resulted in the ship being set against the dock before reaching her proper position with her stem close up against the stern of the ship ahead. The near corner of the dock touched the ship's side at the sea ladder (*E*). The wooden guard rail along the water line took up the slight shock without injury. A gentle kick of the outboard engine sent us ahead into correct position—the guard rail sliding against the piles. When we left this dock the current again was flooding and no captain offered objection to having a tug tow him out against it into the river.

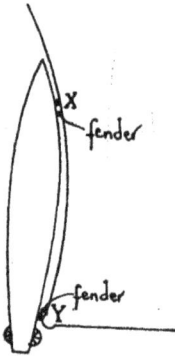

Fig. 54—Fall River Line steamer dock.

Once a landing was made at Fall River alongside a curving dock designed for a large side-wheel steamer to fit against (Fig. 54). To avoid resting against the propeller guard, the stern was allowed to project about ten yards beyond the end of the dock. The group of piles there came against the ship's side just forward of the guard. The edge of the forecastle deck rested against a raised part of the dock, built specially to meet the projecting guard rail of the Fall River steamers. Several fenders were used at each point of contact with the dock. What first appeared to be rather a difficult situation gave us a good berth.

At the navy yard six lines, three forward and three aft, usually are used. Before commencing a dock trial get out three or four more lines. Run them in directions along which it is calculated the heaviest pull will be. Put the outboard engine ahead and the inboard engine astern. Start them very slowly and keep them at about the same speeds, so that the ahead and astern impulses are neutralized. This is easy to say, but hard to do. After a long overhaul the engines will be very stiff, particularly if much turbine work has been done. It probably will take quite a jolt of steam to move them. Unless the engineers are very careful, this will result in some violent surges back and forth. After both engines are running steadily, readjust the lines so that the strain is divided equally among three or four lines and the pull on each is distributed equally among all its parts. Station an officer on the bridge to ring "stop" on the annunciators should a line part or other craft be drawn into the screw currents. Have a man aft watching for floating logs or other obstructions which may be sucked into the propellers. Work up gradually to about 120 turns. That is plenty to serve the purpose of the trial.

If it is desired to reverse the engines, bring the bow well in against the dock, so there is at least five yards between the inboard propeller and its edge. Readjust the lines in accordance with the changed directions of pull. Start the engines slowly. If a line should part with the inboard engine going ahead and the outboard engine backing, the inboard propeller would soon come against the dock with very sad results. Therefore, it is recommended that this part of the trial be very brief and that the engines be limited to low speeds.

CHAPTER XV

ANCHORING

When anchoring singly in a designated berth decide upon two accurately located objects ashore which are suitable for fixing the positions of the ship during the approach and for determining when the anchor should be let go. The angle between the two objects should be at least 60 degrees and as near 90 degrees as practicable, but it is even more important that both of them be accurately fixed on the chart. On several occasions we relied upon bearings of a prominent cliff at Gonaives, Haiti. It seemed as if the resultant position did not check as well as it might with that of other vessels. The same idea occurred to one of our seniors, and we were induced to look somewhat closer into the matter. Ultimately it developed that the chart in the vicinity of this cliff was only a realistic piece of free-hand sketching.

Determine the bearings of the two objects from the center of the assigned berth. Bring one object on the correct bearing and head toward it. Adjust the course a few degrees to right or left to keep on this bearing. If there is a current across your course, it may be necessary to head quite a bit from the bearing, so that the resultant track will be along it. An officer should be assigned to the duty of taking bearings on this object and reporting them about every ten seconds. Another takes bearings on the second object when you near the assigned berth. Lay off along the reverse course from the center of the berth a distance of fifty yards to find the position of the bridge when the anchor should be let go and the correct bearing of the second object at that time. The distance from compass to anchor is thirty yards and twenty more are added to allow for the distance the ship travels from the time the navigator says he is on the bearing until the anchor is let go. Reduce speed early in the approach and stop when about three hundred yards from the berth. This will give a 2- to 3-knot headway when it is reached. Let go on the corrected bearing and back one-third both engines. This will bring the ship dead in the water when you have from twenty-five to thirty-five fathoms of chain at the water's edge. If the water is ten fathoms or less, secure the chain wherever it happens to be, between these limits, when the ship loses headway. This allows a different part of the chain to be painted daily and distributes the wear over more links.

It is permissible to anchor with the wind from any direction unless it is of gale force or there is a heavy sea. You may anchor with a current from astern unless it exceeds three knots, but use the anchor whose chain will not ride across your stem and let the strain come on it gradually. When the current is over three knots it is highly advisable to turn into it before anchoring. We once watched a destroyer anchor with a 5-knot current from astern in the Yangtze off Kiukiang, and do not recommend such procedure. It puts a tremendous strain on the chain and may drag the anchor out of the assigned berth.

Destroyers may anchor very effectively in division formation. This used to be the normal procedure of the Asiatic Destroyer Squadron at Chefoo. On signal from the division commander speed was reduced to two-thirds when about 1,000 yards from the assigned anchorages. "Speed zero" was executed when this distance was reduced to about 400 yards. The signal to anchor was hauled down when the flagship was in her proper berth. Two-thirds astern on both engines was required to bring the ships to a stop with thirty fathoms of chain out. It is necessary to maintain quite a high rate of speed right up to the time of anchoring, due to the great difficulty of position keeping at low speeds. For this reason one-third speed should not be used during the approach.

In the Yangtze it is usual to moor with two anchors to prevent the yaw caused by the 5-knot current. Approach the anchorage against the current and stop from one-third speed about fifty yards beyond the selected spot. When you are going ahead through the water at about three knots—actually two knots downstream—and you are in the proper berth again, let go the starboard anchor (*A*, Fig. 55). Ease out sixty fathoms of chain slowly and drift down with the current (*B*), kicking ahead an engine occasionally to let the chain take the strain gently. Ride to the anchor and swing left with rudder and engines until the chain tends about 20 degrees on the starboard bow. Then drop the port anchor (*C*). Kick ahead the port engine one-third, heave in the starboard chain to forty-five fathoms, and ease out on the port chain sufficiently to keep both chains taut (*D*). The ship then is held in an absolutely steady position.

Anchors should be sighted every three days to prevent them from being buried in the silt or the shifting sands. One engine and one boiler used to be routine for sighting anchors. When heaving in against a strong current always take the strain off the chain by kicking an engine ahead.

The routine of sighting anchors often will not prevent them from being buried in the banks of sand which shift along the river's bottom. On one occasion we started to sight anchors after they had been down three days. The downstream anchor was hauled clear without difficulty. But when we tried to bring up the other the chain came up and down with the 30-fathom mark at the water's edge. The lead indicated eight fathoms—sandy bottom. The anchor and twenty-two fathoms of chain had been buried in the sand. The ship was yawed right and left with rudder and engines. Foot by foot we pulled the chain out of the sand. After two hours of tugging we had eight fathoms at the water's edge and not another inch could we get. We secured the chain with all the stoppers on board and rode with it up and down all day. Even this terrific strain had no effect and in the late afternoon we eased out the chain again,

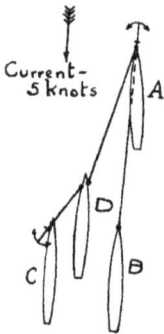

Fig. 55.— Mooring in the Yangtze at Hankow.

dropped the other anchor—a very bad mistake, as events proved—and moored in our original position.

During the next day arrangements were made with Chinese divers to try to recover the anchor. When they arrived to try their skill we found that the downstream anchor also could not be budged, though it had been down only forty hours. We put increasingly heavy strains on this chain and finally it parted. The ship was worked up over the upstream anchor and the chain brought up and down. A weak-looking little Chinaman then took a deep breath and slid down the chain, without any equipment or even a line. After remaining down for a long time, during which we also held our breath, the daring adventurer came up from his "twenty thousand leagues under the sea." He reported that the chain disappeared into a bank of sand, a handful of which he showed us as proof. He had not been able to find the anchor itself. Considering the very muddy water and strong current this seemed to us almost an incredible feat of diving. It could hardly have been faked in any way, for our contract was "no anchor—no money." However, we considered ourselves sufficiently under moral obligation to the diver to give him $10—probably the easiest money he had ever earned.

All that day and the next we rode with the chain up and down, hoping that this pull might eventually work the anchor loose. And, "if eventually," we hoped, "why not now?" If the chain had parted we would have had a pleasant job during the remainder of our stay at Hankow—going ahead one-third speed to keep in our assigned berth. However, we broke about even in our luck—the anchor held and so did the chain. The next day we were ordered to proceed to Kiukiang, and our only anchor insisted on remaining at Hankow.

The division commander directed the *Pope* to give us an anchor. The transfer of this anchor was a problem not without its interest (Fig. 56). Our ship, the *John D. Ford*, rode to the starboard anchor with 40 fathoms of chain on deck. The *Pope* made an excellent, though difficult, landing along our starboard side (Position *A*). The *Pope's* port anchor was then hoisted over on the *Ford's* starboard billboard. Forty-five fathoms of the *Pope's* port chain were run over and laid out on the *Ford's* forecastle. This completed the *Pope's* part of the exchange. It remained for us to shift over the riding chain to the *Pope*.

We ran our heavy bullnose stopper through the bullnose and secured its large pelican hook to the riding chain outside the ship. The deck stoppers were then knocked off and the chain eased out until the strain came on the bullnose stopper. This held for a few minutes while we were making arrangements for the next move. But then the pelican hook opened out and let the chain run through with a terrifying clatter. The *Ford* went ahead one-third both engines to take the strain off the chain. Although the pelican hook had gripped again after letting a few fathoms run through it was thought best not to let the strain come on the riding chain again.

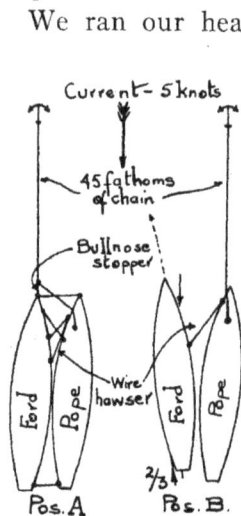

FIG. 56.—Transferring anchor chain in the Yangtze.

In consequence the *Ford* maneuvered with engines and rudder—assisted by the *Pope's* rudder—to hold the ships over the anchor until the maneuver had been completed. An officer was posted in the eyes of the ship to indicate the tend of the chain and the degree of strain on it. One engine was kept steady at one-third ahead. The other was kicked ahead occasionally as necessary to hold the ship against the current. This was continued for about an hour until the transfer of the chain was finally effected.

The *Ford's* riding chain was unshackled at forty-five fathoms. Its end was cleared away from our forecastle and passed in through the *Pope's* port anchor chock. It was then shackled to her port chain, thus replacing the forty-five fathoms she had given us (Position *A*). All that remained now was to get clear. A wire hawser was led from our midship chock, just forward of the midship deck house, well forward on the *Pope's* forecastle. All the *Pope's* lines were singled and kept in hand. The pelican hook of our bullnóse stopper was tripped and the *Pope* rode to the anchor. Just as the strain was coming on the chain, all the *Pope's* lines were cast off and the *Ford* rode to her wire hawser (Position *B*). Our bow was swept out by the current. We went ahead two-thirds with the outboard engine and cast off the hawser. We were clear immediately. While running down the river to Kiukiang the chain was connected up to our new starboard anchor. After a time we will resume this tale and tell something of our experiences at Kiukiang.

One lesson these experiences taught was the tremendous strength of the chains issued to destroyers. A destroyer captain need have no fear of one parting. Even if he should deliberately try to break one, he will find it quite a job.

Our negotiations with the Chinese diver at Hankow had a sequel, which, if perhaps not very instructive, is at least sufficiently amusing. The next winter at Manila we received a despatch from Hankow asking if it were true that we had made an agreement with a Chinese diver that he should have half the value of our anchor if he could recover it. While we had not contemplated anything at the time but immediate recovery, none of us could remember having specified any definite time limit when the contract, oral of course, should become void. Technically at least our contract still held. So we replied to that effect. It seems that the Chinaman had waited until the river went down about fifty feet, organized a search of the dry river bed, and dug the anchor out of the sand. Doubtless some destroyer captain was glad to get that anchor the next summer, and the Chinaman had received the reward due his industry. "Ill blows the wind that profits nobody."

When anchored in a dangerous position it is essential to

know immediately when a ship begins to drag. This may occur in two ways. The anchor may break loose altogether or pull foot by foot through the bottom. When it drags in a strong current it will come loose entirely. Then, as it is pulled over the bottom, the ship will be shaken so severely that everyone on board will know what has happened. Once we were anchored in Kashiwabara Wan along the edge of a 5-knot current. The holding ground was poor—alternate rocky ledges and beds of sand. The depth of water was about four fathoms and we had thirty fathoms of chain out. For about a week the anchor held perfectly. Then one afternoon an eddy caught the ship and swung it broadside to the current. The anchor broke loose with a terrific jar. We were all in the wardroom and there was no doubt in the mind of anybody as to what had happened. A rush for the forecastle ensued. But before we could get there the other anchor had been let go by the extra man kept on watch for that specific purpose. This anchor brought us to about fifty yards short of a Japanese destroyer. To avoid a recurrence of such incidents we went in where the water was much less in depth and the current greatly reduced in force. For several weeks we lay in two and one-half fathoms. While anchoring in such shallow water, particularly with a rocky bottom, is normally not good procedure, it was in this case a proper choice between two evils. Here again Scylla was thought less dangerous than Charybdis.

On another occasion Division 43 anchored in formation in the Yangtze off Anking. The city is located on the outboard side of a sharp curve in the river. The current was very strong along the city bank and had scoured out the bottom so that the water was deep and the holding ground poor. Within five minutes all four ships were dragging rapidly down the river. Unfortunately the engines had been secured and we had to wait for several minutes before they were again available. During this time the anchor had been plowing a deep furrow along the bottom. We next anchored across the river from the city. Here we were on the inboard side of the curve, the current was weaker and silt had made the water comparatively shallow. Here the holding ground was good and we found no difficulty in getting the anchor to grip. The *Truxtun* while dragging down had the misfortune to hook a large obstruction. After dragging this along the bottom for several hours her chain broke.

Having related several incidents which occurred at later dates, let us now return to the situation which confronted the *John D. Ford* at Kiukiang. We were instructed to remain there for a week. Off the foreign concession the bottom was covered with a layer of large, smoothly polished boulders. The Asiatic pilot warned that this was very poor holding ground and that vessels frequently dragged with two anchors down—we had only one. This not only decreased the holding power, but would allow the ship to yaw with the current. This in turn increased the pull on the anchor, by putting the ship at an angle with the current, and tended to break the anchor out, by continually pulling it from side to side. Well knowing all our dangers, we anchored with extreme caution. But no sooner had we taken a strain on the chain than the ship began to yaw through an arc of 40 degrees and the chain vibrated so violently that it shook the whole ship. This gave a very decided impression that the anchor was dragging, one which was reënforced by the pessimistic vein of the Asiatic pilot. After some discussion it was decided to sight the anchor. When the chain came up polished like silver, it was easy to guess that the vibrations of the chain had been caused by dragging over the rocks. The anchor held perfectly during our entire stay. The underlying idea of *Sailing Directions* and *Pilots* seems to be that every possible danger must be warned against, so that in case of accident their writers cannot be charged with neglect. Thus, while these warnings should be given consideration, they should not be taken too seriously. Rely chiefly on your own experience and your own estimate of the situation on the ground, remembering that nothing is ever as dangerous as the report of it.

When a vessel is riding into a strong wind and heavy sea, with considerable roll, yaw, and pitch, the anchor may be pulled slowly along a sandy bottom. This is rather difficult to detect. There is no vibration of the anchor chain nor jar to the ship. Naturally a drift lead is no use when the ship is yawing one hundred yards from side to side. Bearings of points ashore change so slowly that the officer taking them will assume a personal error, a slight change in the compass, or a different part of the yaw. This assumption is even more probable when there are no lights ashore and bearings must be taken on points dimly visible in the light of moon or stars, or even on the lights of another ship which is herself yawing through a wide arc. During our month in the Kurile Islands every possible precaution was taken to check the position of the ship during the night. Still one night we dragged one hundred yards toward the beach in a heavy storm without detecting it until dayligh.

Never try to anchor a destroyer on a steep bank. The northern shore of Corregidor rises very steeply out of the water. It drops away almost as sharply underwater to a depth of thirty-five fathoms. During the last phase of a typhoon the Asiatic Destroyer Squadron tried to anchor in the lee of the island. The wind was force-seven. The rain was blinding—that is not a figure of speech. Night was falling. The water in the lee was calm. We ran in close to the land and let go the anchor and sixty fathoms of chain in twenty-five fathoms of water. As soon as the strain came on, the anchor rolled down the slope. We hove in the chain until there was twelve fathoms at the water's edge. Leaving the anchor hanging thus under foot we approached the shore gradually at another place, just avoiding a mooring buoy in the darkness and rain. When the anchor touched we eased out to forty-five fathoms. Again the anchor pulled off. We then gave up attempting to anchor on the bank and let go in thirty-five fathoms where the bottom was level. With sixty fathoms out the anchor held perfectly. By this time it was about 2100. Just as we were settled for the night the order came for the squadron to proceed into Manila. We piled into that small harbor at 0100 in one beautiful meleé. Oh, what a night!

Under ordinary conditions of wind and current two destroyers may ride to one anchor. This was the usual practice in Manila during the winter months. Where there is a strong current, as in the North River, this plan will not work. Once two reduced-commissioned destroyers, secured together, were carried down rapidly from 182d Street with the current. Luckily we had enough clear space below us to quickly warm the engines of one of the destroyers and get under way on one boiler before coming into contact with other vessels. For two hours we maneuvered about the river, trying out all the best anchorages. Finally the anchor held with ninety fathoms of chain out.

To avoid such difficulties a novel plan was used by the Scouting Fleet destroyers. Two destroyers anchored abreast of each other fifty yards apart. They were then brought together by use of the rudder and secured. After riding that way for a week an attempt was made to heave up one of the anchors preparatory to getting under way. The two anchors were found hooked together with the chains wound around them. It took several hours to clear away this tangle. We mention this plan only to show that it was not a good one.

Not nearly enough advantage is taken of the ability of destroyers to anchor in the open sea. This can be done in waters up to thirty-five fathoms or in winds up to force-six. Throughout the fine weather in the summer months off the Atlantic coast a destroyer can anchor practically anywhere. During the reserve cruises last year we anchored probably fifteen times in the open sea, off Fire Island, Shinnecock, Cape Cod, and Martha's Vineyard. On night trips from Newport to New York our practice was to anchor about 2300 off Shinnecock or Fire Island and get under way at 0600. On trips from New York to Newport we would anchor in Gardner's Bay about 2000 and get under way at 0700. This practice gave all hands a fine night's sleep and met with much approval.

There seems to be a similar disinclination to lie to in the open sea. The ship will ride easily with the wind and sea about 20 degrees abaft the beam. You can let a boiler die out and partly

secure the engines. It frequently is convenient to lie to thus
when acting as a plane guard, when you want to take a recess
during drills for lunch, or where it is necessary to maintain a
definite station and the water is too deep for anchoring. When
making mail trips from Gonaives to Guantanamo we used to
lie to in the calm Haitian waters so we could fully enjoy our
moving pictures on the forecastle. Always give your people
such little pleasures as destroyer life affords and reduce the
steaming watches to a minimum in tropical waters.

Chapter XVI

SECURING TO A BUOY

If you know the system it is a simple matter to secure to a buoy in any wind or current. But the first few times you try it, you may be reminded of that curious saying attributed to Clausewitz that it is the simple which is difficult.

When about eight hundred yards from the buoy stop and lower the motor launch. In addition to the regular crew, send a nimble seaman along to assist in connecting your lines and chain to the buoy. Approach the buoy at one-third speed. When about three hundred yards from it stop the engines and coast up to it with barely steerage way on the ship.

If there is neither wind nor current to be considered, head about three yards to that side of the buoy which is most convenient for handling lines and chain. When the stem is about twenty-five yards from the buoy, with one to two knots headway on the ship, back one-third both engines. Stop them so that the buoy is touching the side under the billboard with the ship dead in the water. The motor launch should then run alongside the buoy and help in handling the lines.

Run a mooring line with a big hook in the end down through the anchor chain chock. Hook it into the shackle on the buoy. Heave in the line with the capstan and when taut secure it to the bitts used for No. 2 mooring line. Meanwhile a 3½-inch line has been shackled to the end of the anchor chain and passed out through the bullnose to the buoy. The man on the buoy passes it through the ring on the buoy and throws the end up on deck again. When the buoy is in its proper position, and not until then, a man in the eyes of the ship takes all the turns out of this chain line, passes its end through the bullnose, and takes it to the capstan. While heaving in on this line let the chain run out easily. Its end will be hauled through the buoy ring and up through the bullnose. Secure it with a deck stopper, throw off the hook rope, and hoist the affirmative.

The use of the motor launch, while a wise precaution, is not essential. If you have a large, flat buoy it is a simple matter to land a man on the buoy from the forecastle. Even with the small can-shaped buoys, it is not difficult to secure without a boat. The man on the buoy should always wear a life belt and be a good swimmer.

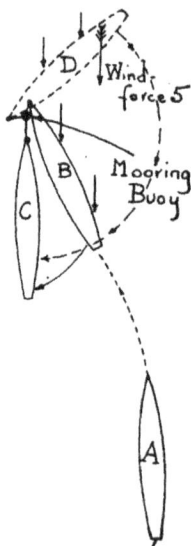

FIG. 57.—Securing to a buoy in a strong wind.

If the wind is strong (Fig. 57), head well to the windward of the buoy during the approach (A). In the latter part of the approach try to bring the wind about 30 degrees on one bow and the buoy an equal amount on the other. Allow the ship to be blown down on the buoy until it comes against the side under the billboard (B). Secure the hook rope quickly and heave it taut to prevent the buoy from getting past your stem to the weather bow. Secure the chain and drop down into position C. Another equally good method is to approach with the wind about 30 degrees on the quarter as in position D. A landing in any position between B and D is satisfactory as long as the buoy is against your lee bow. The bow will then become a pivot, about which the ship will swing into position C, getting there just about the time your chain is secured. Even a strong breeze is not a disadvantage in securing to a buoy— as long as you keep the buoy tight against your lee bow. It is well, however, to make ample allowance against being carried to leeward, for then all you can do is to back off and try it again.

When there is a current (Fig. 58), bring it about 30 degrees on one bow during the approach and the buoy an equal amount on the other (*A*). Make very ample allowance for the current effect, or it will sweep you down past the buoy. Get your bow somewhat above the buoy and let the current sweep it down gradually upon it. To prevent the buoy getting past your stem, try to bring it against the side opposite the gun, rather than under the billboard. Let the ship go aft slowly and hold the hook rope when the buoy is under the billboard (*B*). While the chain is being secured the ship will drop back into position *C*.

The approach may also be made with the current 30 degrees on the quarter (*D*) or from any direction between *B* and *D*. But be sure—at the risk of frequent repetition—to allow enough for the current, for you must bring the buoy against your lee bow and hold it there. Landings have been made frequently with a 3-knot current on the quarter. If the mooring crew is well trained, the chain will be secured before the ship swings head into the current. If you get swept past the buoy in a with-the-current landing, you are very much out of luck—so again allow enough for the current. With all these warnings I'll bet Ole Man River fools you the first time you try this landing.

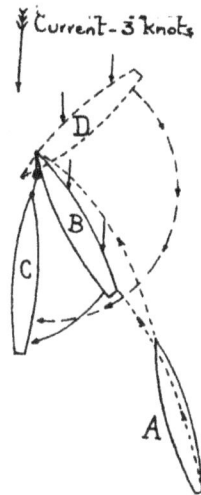

Fig. 58.—Securing to a buoy in a strong current.

At Shanghai it is customary to secure bow and stern to two buoys. With the usual 3-knot tidal current, it is desirable to approach the buoys against it. Secure the bow to one buoy in the usual manner, remembering that the other will be close under your stern. Then have the motor launch run a heavy wire hawser to the buoy astern. If several destroyers secure to one pair of buoys all should run their wire lines to the buoy astern, as a heavy strain will come on them when the tide changes.

Once we came into Shanghai at exactly slack water with a force-five breeze blowing at right angles to the line of buoys

(Fig. 59). There was no difficulty in coming alongside the buoy (*A*) and securing the chain in the usual manner. But by the time this had been accomplished the wind had blown the stern across the river (*B*). A wire hawser with a mooring line tied to its end was run from the fantail to the buoy astern by the motor launch. The ship was twisted with the engines to bring the stern up against the wind toward this buoy. Slack was taken in on the wire to hold every yard gained. It took some thirty minutes of maneuvering and untold gallons of oil to bring the ship into position *C*. It would have been far preferable to have gone farther up the river and anchored until the tide started to flood. Then after the bow had been secured to the buoy, the ship would have taken position *D* instead of *B* and it would have been easy to bring her into position *C* for securing. Sometimes, where a slight strain only is required, an after mooring line can be hooked to the messenger used for hoisting boats and the stern hove in by the capstan. This method would not have been effective in the above cases.

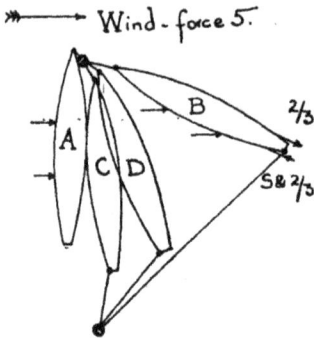

FIG. 59.—Securing to two mooring buoys in the Wangpoo at Shanghai.

Chapter XVII

TOWING A LARGE SHIP

A large aircraft tender lay at anchor on the narrow shelf along the western shore of Cozumel Island (Fig. 60). It was heading parallel to the coast and riding into the Gulf Stream (Position X). A norther came up during the morning watch and by 0800 the wind was blowing force-five from the starboard beam. It was dangerous to go ahead from her anchorage because the wind might blow her into the shoal water before sufficient headway could be gotten on the ship. Also a destroyer A was lying in her line of advance. To clear this line of advance the destroyer got under way in the short time of sixteen minutes. Just before moving, this destroyer had offered to give the tender a tow and had commenced making preparations to get out her towing hawser. The second boiler was cut in just as the anchor was aweigh. The ship was turned sharply to the right into position B. Then effort was made to twist her to the left to gain a favorable position for pulling out the tender's bow, so as to point her clear. But here we reckoned without the current. This was only moderate over the shallow coral shelf, but out over the 100-fathom line it was a good three knots. This acted against the twisting effect of

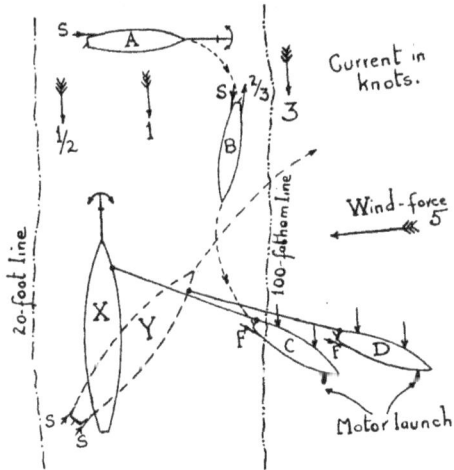

Fig. 60.—Towing an aircraft tender off Cozumel.

the destroyer's engines and largely balanced it. It had been intended originally to twist the ship about 135 degrees to the left from position *B*, while still keeping in the same location. However, when a twist of 45 degrees had been effected the bow projected out into the deep water where the full effect of the current was felt. The strong wind also exerted unfavorable pressure against the port bow. Thus not even full twisting effect—starboard engine full ahead, port engine full astern—could bring the ship around more than about 70 degrees from position *B*. Also, the ship was being swept down bodily from a position on the tender's bow to her beam.

While the destroyer was maneuvering the tender sent over with a large motor launch the end of an 8-inch manila hawser. This was brought through the destroyer's stern chock and secured around the base of the antiaircraft gun on the fantail. By the time this was done—only ten minutes from the instant the destroyer's anchor was aweigh—she had been carried by the current into position *C*. Towing was commenced immediately. To try to push the destroyer's head to the left against the current, or at least to maintain the present position, full left rudder was used and the starboard engine was sent ahead by steps to full speed.

As soon as strain came on the towing hawser the tender weighed both her anchors. To increase the pull the destroyer's port engine was put ahead one-third, but the bow commenced swinging to the right and this engine had to be stopped. Our motor launch was used as a tug, pushing against our starboard bow. About ten minutes of towing pulled the tender through an arc of about 40 degrees (*Y*). She was then pointed well clear of the shoals and went ahead full speed—sixteen knots. Just as she was about to cut the towing hawser it parted at her chock. She continued ahead and easily cleared the shoals. The destroyer was in position *D* when the hawser parted. After heaving it in, she reanchored in the tender's berth. This maneuver is not cited as an example of the best methods of towing. Rather it is used to illustrate that old saying: "The

best is the enemy of the good." Time was of vital importance
and what we all wanted was a plan which would produce the
results in the shortest time. Our
method met this requirement, though
a much better one could have been used
had unlimited time been available.

Fig. 61 gives an idea of such a better
plan. The destroyer A is in a favorable
position for towing on the bow of the
tender X. She is headed in a good direction—halfway between wind and current. The towing hawser is led through
the chock on the port side abreast the
searchlight platform, thus permitting

FIG. 61.—A better method
of towing had time been
available.

the strain of towing to be divided between the two engines and
giving complete control of the ship with the rudder.

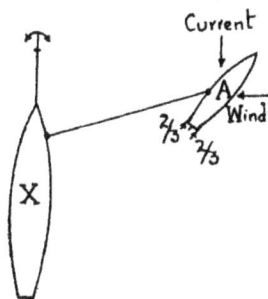

CHAPTER XVIII

HANDLING A DESTROYER IN HEAVY WEATHER
AND AMONG FIELD ICE

In a long heavy sea with wind force-eight to nine a destroyer pointed into the waves with the engines making turns for five knots will keep her forecastle practically dry. The bow will rise beautifully to meet each mountainous wave and its crest will fall just a foot or two short of gaining the forecastle deck. Occasionally the ship will fall off from the wind a bit and take a tremendous roll. We registered one of 52 degrees one night of a gale off the Kurile Islands. As I lay on the deck of the emergency cabin tangled in coats and blankets and almost buried under a deluge of navigational books it seemed for a few seconds that we had capsized. But this roll was the exception, for usually the motion of the ship was easy and gentle. For one daylight period during this storm, to gain distance toward our destination, we brought the wind 10 degrees abaft the beam and increased speed to fifteen knots. The ship behaved much better than we had expected. Occasionally heavy rolls up to 35 degrees were experienced, but the normal motion did not exceed 15 degrees. No dangerously heavy seas came on board. During this storm the barometer held steady at 28.83 for sixty hours.

A destroyer does not ride so well in a short sea, which may form in restricted waters or when a strong wind is blowing against a current. Off the Kii promontory, the Hatteras of Japan, the ship was forced one evening into a force-seven to eight wind. The Japanese current was running three knots against the wind. This combination produced a very short and violent sea. Even though we reduced speed ultimately to eight knots, every wave sent solid sheets of spray over the tops of the stacks. Once we got out of the full force of the current the sea moderated. Later in the same location a heavier storm was encountered. But this time the wind was with the current and the sea was longer—the ship, in consequence, rode much easier.

When running into a head sea lighten the bow by pumping out the forward oil tanks. Reduce speed, if necessary, to five knots. Damage to the forward bulkhead of the chart house and the bridge may confidently be expected if this is not done in time. At the first sign of rough weather pull up the metal shutters to protect the non-shatterable glass windows. For, whatever their guarantee, a fine white-capped sea will shatter them into a hundred pieces. We saw this done to four windows by a single wave.

When leaving port in bad weather be sure to get the forecastle well secured before you enter rough water. See that the metal covers are fitted tightly over the chain pipes which lead to the lockers. It is not pleasant to see one being washed about the forecastle by sportive waves, which meanwhile are filling the chain lockers, and probably the paint locker also. It is well to have all life lines reported rigged and secured whenever the ship gets under way. In rough weather have extra life lines rigged inboard of the torpedo tubes. It is good practice to run a line between the upper ends of the two anchor stocks to hold the anchors steady against the impact of the seas.

When riding out a typhoon at anchor forty-five fathoms of chain is ample if the water is less than ten fathoms and the holding ground is good. More chain greatly increases the yaw of the ship and it is this continual pulling of the anchor from side to side which causes it to drag. Have the shackle on deck just inside the stopper, so that the chain can be slipped quickly in case of emergency. Have a $3\frac{1}{2}$-inch line made fast to the chain with a torpedo buoy at the end to facilitate the recovery of the chain, if it should be slipped. While the dropping of a second anchor underfoot would stop the yaw, this would make it very difficult for the ship to get under way quickly during a storm. For this reason it is not recommended. To prevent wear on the chain ease out a few feet every watch, so that

different links will wear against the chock. The use of engines
to reduce the strain on the chain is not recommended. In case
of necessity they can be used to keep the strain off the chain
entirely, maintaining position by means of the anchor buoy.
This procedure is impracticable in the blinding rain which
accompanies a typhoon.

Getting under way in a heavy sea requires skillful shiphan-
dling. I have a vivid recollection of a terrible night in Cod Bay,
Shimushu. The April gale we were riding out had shifted 180
degrees. The fine lee we had rejoiced in during the day was
anything but a lee after the storm center passed with its
reversal of wind. A force-seven breeze now was blowing our
stern directly toward the breakers only 150 yards off. The temperature was about 25 degrees and we were literally frozen.
In the brilliant moonlight those breakers, as the hours wore on,
seemed to get nearer and nearer. About 3:00 A.M., when
courage is supposed to be lowest, we decided to get under way.
As our splendid boatswain's mate and his little forecastle gang
went out in that icy blast to heave in and cat the anchor my
heart went out to them. It was realized that some skillful
handling of the ship would be necessary. We could not let the
anchor hang over the side in that storm and to get it on the
billboard would take some minutes. During these minutes we
could not let the ship be carried around broadside to the wind
for fear of being blown on the lee shore. Likewise we could not
get too much headway on the ship lest waves and spray come
over the men working on the anchor. Finally, we could not
keep those people out in the icy wind while we waited for
favorable opportunities.

As the ship was yawing considerably it was important that
the anchor come aweigh as she was headed directly into the
wind. This purpose was accomplished at the expense of a few
seconds' delay. Our next task was to keep the ship pointed into
the wind with the least possible headway. As the bow started
to fall off to one side that engine was kicked ahead one-third
and full rudder used to bring the ship back. In this way the

ship was kept headed into the wind with not over three knots headway. Consequently no spray came over the forecastle until the anchor had been secured on the billboard. This, despite darkness and a slippery deck, was done in record time. After the forecastle had been secured we went ahead one-third speed both engines directly into the wind until day broke— getting about one hour of magnificent sleep.

A destroyer seldom will be required to skirt an ice field at night. However, the very infrequency of such experiences makes it desirable to record the lessons learned from them. From February to April the enormous ice fields which form in the Sea of Okhotsk are forced out through the gaps in the southern part of the Kurile chain into the Pacific. We fortunately first encountered the field about 1500 and were able to develop a method of skirting it before darkness came on. The ice was about 20 feet thick. Its surface was very rough and uneven, but the recent calm weather had resulted in the field being frozen again into a solid mass. There were no breaks or lanes through the ice. The edges of the field, however, were very irregular. There were deep bays and long promontories. A fringe of small pieces of ice and small bergs extended out for about 150 yards from the edge of the solid ice. Many of these pieces would have bent a propeller blade. Along the edge of this fringe the temperature of the sea water was 28 degrees— out about 1,000 yards it increased to 30 degrees.

After nightfall we continued skirting the field, trying to keep about 250 yards from the edge of the solid ice. The moon was out; the sky was partly cloudy. When the moon shone through the gaps in the clouds the field could be seen very dimly and uncertainly at about 1,000 yards, but it was difficult to judge the distance it was away. The temperature of the sea water was reported by the engine-room every fifteen minutes and this gave a good indication as to our distance from the field. The fringe of small pieces gave the last and surest indication. These pieces could be seen about fifty yards ahead of the bow and often it was necessary to resort to maneuvering to avoid hitting one with the stem or a propeller.

In following the very irregular edge of the field frequent changes of course were necessary. Sometimes the field was seen in the moonlight far on the outboard bow and course had to be altered 90 degrees, or even more. A second destroyer kept position about 1,000 yards outside us. All our changes of course were signaled to her by flashing light. While the moon was out ten knots was found a suitable speed. After it went down, five knots was all that seemed safe. After this experience it was made normal practice to report the temperature of the sea water every fifteen minutes at night or in a fog whenever the ship was under way in the vicinity of ice. When the temperature dropped below 30 degrees speed was reduced and caution was the watchword.

CHAPTER XIX

HANDLING BOATS

The hoisting of a boat on a destroyer is almost inevitably heralded by a long series of wild shouts: "Heave round," "Avast heaving," etc. We resolved to avoid this unseamanlike clamor. Finally, after several months, we proved to our people that a boat could be hoisted silently. The usual hand signals were adopted for use. The boatswain's mate in charge leaned out over the side just forward of the davits and signaled his orders to a man at the after end of the forecastle. The latter repeated the signal to the man at the capstan. Control was far quicker and more accurate than when the word was passed along the deck. At night a system of flash-light signals proved equally effective. Having worked this miracle, we took courage in our hands and devised a system to short-circuit that familiar shout: "Pump up the gravity tank"—but that momentous question hardly comes within the scope of "handling boats."

In hoisting the motor launch the forward fall should be hooked on with the hook pointing forward. Then, if the boat is lowered in a rough sea, the fall can easily be unhooked I once saw a boat lowered in Newport in quite a sea when this simple rule was violated. It took several minutes to unhook the fall. A chief petty officer first tried it and had his hand so badly smashed that he went to the hospital as quickly as we could get him there. An officer tried next and exactly the same thing happened to him. We have never hooked a fall that way since.

While we were touring the Kurile Islands, our people seemed more anxious to set foot on those inhospitable shores and walk over snow mountains twenty feet high than to make a liberty in New York. One afternoon a recreation party pulled the whaleboat in to the beach at Kashiwabara Wan. Suddenly an onshore breeze sprang up. All attempts to launch the boat through the surf proved unavailing. All hands were soaked in the 30-degree sea water and faced the cheery prospect of spending the night ashore in a deserted fisherman's hut. Our executive officer remembered that we carried a line-throwing gun. Scouting Fleet destroyers now carry a form of rifle bomb which serves the same purpose. A line was quickly shot ashore from the motor launch and the whaleboat towed out through the surf. Its drenched crew upon their return to the ship found themselves for once in an exceptional status as regards the Eighteenth Amendment.

One evening we were lying off Cozumel Island. A force-four wind was blowing on shore. The sea was moderate—rough enough to make hoisting a motor launch quite a risky stunt. The *Wright* was under way off the anchorage. Three of her boats had come to us to secure. We tied them up astern, one behind the other, with a 5-inch mooring line. This line led over the first two boats, which were large motor launches, and was made fast to the hoisting rings in the bow of the third boat, which was a 24-foot motor launch, the same as that used by destroyers. There were about five yards between boats. One of the men on watch made frequent inspections of these boats and the officer with the day's duty did so at hourly intervals.

About 0130, just a few minutes after the officer had made his inspection, it was discovered that the rear boat had disappeared. As the hawser went down vertically over the stern of the second boat, it was evident that the boat had sunk. The first and second boats were hauled up to the ship in turn, secured to separate mooring lines, cast off from the original mooring line, and allowed to ride well astern of the ship. This resulted in the sunken boat resting on the bottom about twenty yards astern of the ship, with a mooring line made fast to her bow. The water was about six fathoms deep. The line was led forward on the starboard side. There was some difficulty getting it under the propeller, but a yaw of the ship finally brought it clear. The line was brought through an amidship chock and hauled in with the messenger to the capstan until the boat was on the bottom about under the davits. A large snatch block was secured to the head of the forward davit with a wire torpedo strap and shackles. The mooring line was led through the block and hove in with the capstan until the bow of the boat was several feet out of the water. The upper part of the boat was toward the ship and it pounded heavily in the rough sea. Fenders and oars kept any damage from being done. At considerable risk a coxswain got down into the boat and after many efforts succeeded in running a torpedo strap through the forward hoisting ring. The eyes of the strap were shackled together and the forward fall hooked into the shackle. A strain was taken on the fall and the mooring line cast off.

The next problem was to get the after fall hooked. The first idea was to catch the stern with grapnels and bring it up to the surface. While we got several grapnels to catch, it proved impossible to accomplish our purpose. All that remained was to hoist the bow of the boat two blocks and pray that the davit would hold as the sea tossed the boat about. We did so and the davit held. The stern was now about three feet under water. Our coxswain again was lowered down into the boat to try to run a torpedo strap through the after hoisting ring. This, as you will remember, is in a most inaccessible place under the platform in the stern of the boat. It was several feet under water. The boat was being battered about by the sea and pounded against the side. It must have taken half an hour to get that line through the ring. Once through, it was shackled together and the after fall hooked through the shackle. We hove in on the after fall and slacked off the forward fall until the boat was level and even with the deck. The entire damage to the boat was a broken rudder and the boat box, a few life belts, and, some bottom boards missing. The hull was absolutely intact, without even a bad dent or scrape. The entire operation had taken four and one-half hours.

CHAPTER XX

CONCLUSION

We would like again to emphasize the fact that the methods described in this volume are based upon, and proved by, actual experience. However, they must be used with judgment and not blindly followed. Remember that each situation must be estimated independently and on its own merits. We have described type situations only. To each there are endless variations and the necessary modifications must be applied to the methods recommended. Try them out under favorable conditions before putting them to the test in critical situations.

Record the results of every maneuver—the mistakes made and the lessons learned. Get your work down to a system. Develop this so completely that you have an answer to every threat of wind or current and a trick to take you out of every danger. Next will come that spirit of confidence to meet any situation which is half the battle. Then you have arrived as a destroyer captain. Your confidence will permeate down through officers and sailors. Then you will have a ship. When mutual confidence extends through the division, the captains become a "band of brothers." Then you have a division—such a one as followed the little red and white "43" pennant of Commander J. S. Abbott through eastern seas.

The command of a destroyer is the finest job in the world—bar none. If this little volume makes any command more successful and enjoyable or contributes in any degree, however small, toward the efficiency of our destroyer squadrons, its purpose will have been achieved.

www.ingramcontent.com/pod-product-compliance
Lightning Source LLC
Chambersburg PA
CBHW030808100426
42814CB00002B/49